Introduction to
Venture Capital Finance

CHRIS BOVAIRD

Pitman Publishing
128 Long Acre, London WC2E 9AN

A Division of Longman Group UK Limited

First published in 1990

© Longman Group UK Ltd 1990

British Library Cataloguing in Publication Data
Bovaird, Chris
  Introduction to venture capital finance.
  1. Great Britain. Venture capital investment
  I. Title
  332.63

  ISBN 0–273–03215–1

Typeset, printed and bound in Great Britain

Contents

Preface

The venture capital industry in the United Kingdom is the second largest in the world, after that of the United States. Relative to the size of the UK economy, the amount of venture capital available makes the industry the most highly developed in the world. All this has come about in the last fifteen years, prior to which there was no venture capital 'industry' to speak of.

The growth in the number of venture capital firms, volume of capital invested, number of investments, number of companies seeking venture capital and number of companies successfully financed has been remarkable. This remarkable growth has occurred as a result of changing attitudes toward entrepreneurship, small business and enterprise in the UK.

The creation of the Unlisted Securities Market, the Business Expansion Scheme, the Scottish and Welsh Development Agencies are all examples of bodies or schemes established to facilitate the flow of venture capital or similar type finance into the hands of small and entrepreneurial business.

The success of venture capital backed companies (Apple Computers, Tie Rack, Garfunkels Restaurants, Sock Shop) has given venture capital both a glamour and a high profile. Despite this, frequently used buzz-words such as 'seed capital', 'management buy-out', and indeed 'venture capital' itself, are usually misunderstood or not understood at all.

The aim of this book is to provide a basic, factual, university level text book on venture capital finance, and the venture capital industry in the UK. 'Introduction to Venture Capital Finance' is aimed at the reader who wants more than a superficial treatment of venture capital finance as one of the financial world's 'flavours of the month'.

This text is intended for use by entrepreneurs, managers and management trainees in investment management companies, pension management companies, insurance companies, building societies, clearing banks and merchant banks, as well as students in Master of Business Administration (MBA) programmes, and undergraduate (first degree) students of business studies, accountancy, or economics. Its purpose is to provide readers with a sound understanding, based on analysis and fact, of venture capital investment as a rapidly growing source of company finance in the UK.

Statistics are drawn from data prepared by the venture capital industry's principal trade organisations, the British Venture Capital Association (BVCA), and the European Venture Capital Association (EVCA). The analysis is based upon interviews and surveys of practising venture capitalists and of entrepreneurs, conducted by the author during the latter half of 1987 and throughout 1988.

Acknowledgements

This book could not have been written without the aid and assistance of TSB Scotland plc, whose generous sponsorship brought me to the United Kingdom to work, study and teach.

Many former colleagues in the Department of Business and Management at the University of Stirling assisted in many ways both large and small. Catherine Smith, John Beaumont, and Keith Jacques deserve explicit acknowledgement. Thanks also are due to many of the present and former members of the staff of the Scottish Enterprise Foundation.

Philip Ho collaborated with much of the research contained in Part three.

This book is dedicated to Susanne

Part one

Venture capital defined

Venture capital defined – introduction

This book is about venture capital investment. It is important, right from the outset, that the reader has a clear understanding of what the term 'venture capital' and the activity of providing venture capital imply. The first part is therefore concerned with providing the reader with a working knowledge of the subject.

Let us consider first a definition offered by a practitioner. Dr Neil Cross, a Senior Executive with 3i, one of the world's largest and longest established venture capital companies, and a former Chairman of the European Venture Capital Association, described his trade as follows:

> 'the provision of risk bearing capital, usually in the form of a participation in equity, to companies with high growth potential. In addition, the venture capital company provides some value added in the form of management advice and contribution to overall strategy. The relatively high risks for the venture capitalists are compensated by the possibility of high return, usually through substantial capital gains in the medium term.'

The following definition of venture capital investment appeared in the journal of the central bank, The Bank of England Quarterly Bulletin of 1984:

> 'an activity by which investors support entrepreneurial talent with finance and business skills to exploit market opportunities and thus obtain long term capital gains.'

Both definitions seem to agree on the fact that venture capital is a form of investment finance. What makes venture capital distinctive, and what shall be the major themes of Part one, is that venture capital:

- is equity finance;
- requires hands-on management;
- provides superior return through capital gain;
- requires patience.

One often encounters definitions of venture capital investment which reflect the romantic, if not always accurate, view of venture capitalists as backers of boffins at laboratory benches. Many definitions tend to imply a view of venture capital as an activity largely concerned with new products, new technologies, or 'high' technologies. They tend to define venture capital from the perspective of the entrepreneur as inventor.

Other definitions of venture capital investment stress employment generation or entrepreneurial stimulation as key features. These definitions tend to reflect the perspective of the policy makers and social scientists, for whom 'venture capital investment' conjures up images of economic regeneration and small business creation in depressed regions (i.e. venture capital investment as the formula for economic development of the UK).

All of these definitions tend to be full of subjective (and sometimes wishful) thinking. They all see venture capital finance as they would like it to be. This book tries to confine itself to the examination of venture capital as it actually is. As such, it is hoped that the definition which will be used might be enunciated by venture capital investors themselves.

The chapters of Part one consider some of the key managerial and strategic implications of each of the points mentioned above.

2

Venture capital is equity finance

Venture capital is first and foremost, a form of company finance. As such it stands as an alternative or complement to other forms of finance which an entrepreneurial firm may seek or a financial institution may provide. What distinguishes venture capital from other forms of finance is that it is equity based, more participatory, and longer term to maturity. The participation required of the venture capital investor extends beyond the mere provision of capital.

Debt versus equity finance

Broadly speaking, there are just two forms of finance: debt and equity. Financial experts might gasp at this – in their eyes – simplification. There are, of course, as many means of financing a company's growth as there are bankers and merchant bankers to invent them: convertible preferred shares, subordinated debt, capital leases and the like. However, all of these are still only variations or hybrids of the two basic forms of finance, debt and equity and, although this book is not intended to be a primer on finance, it is important, prior to examining the field of venture capital finance, to remind ourselves of the basic attributes and features of debt and equity.

Debt is repayable on a date certain, it bears interest, and tends (by comparison with equity) to be passive. Ordinary equity, on the other hand, has no specific maturity, bears no contractual rate of return, and affords the holder certain rights and privileges which make him (in theory) an active participant in the ownership, management, and profit sharing of the company. Once again, these are generalisations and simplifications, but only so in the aid of clarifying a point.

Debt finance

The most readily recognisable form of debt is a loan, often from a bank or a building society. In the case of, for example, a mortgage loan the lender advances an agreed sum of money. The borrower, in return for receiving finance, contractually agrees to repay the principal, plus accumulated interest, over the stated life of the loan say, 25 years. Prior to advancing funds, the lender will impose certain conditions on the borrower. Typically, these will include the obligation of the homeowner to keep his house insured for replacement value, to maintain the house in a generally good state of repair, and perhaps to install fire or burglar alarms. The lender will impose these conditions because, once the funds have been advanced, he will have little or no control over the day-to-day affairs concerning the house. The local bank manager, as a respected and trusted financial adviser, might be sought for his advice, he may exercise moral persuasion on a borrower to whom he has advanced a large sum of money, but the day-to-day management of, and the homeowner's decisions concerning, the house are outside his legal ability to control. Most important, the lender can exercise no claim to the profits if the owner is lucky enough to sell his house for a capital gain. In this way, the lender may be said to be a 'passive' financier.

Equity finance

Let us now consider the same individual who, having acquired a house in the town, wishes to purchase an income property – a block of flats in an improving neighbourhood in town. Lacking sufficient capital to buy the block on his own, our homeowner approaches his brother. The brother is invited to put up 40% of the capital. The homeowner agrees to be responsible for the day-to-day maintenance of the property, to find tenants, and to handle the cash flows. The brother's responsibility will be to contribute 40% towards the cost of maintenance, insurance, utilities and rates. They agree to sell the block five years into the future and to confer before making major alterations. The homeowner's brother has made an equity investment. Even though he has provided 40% of the finance, he does not expect to be repaid by the homeowner or receive interest on his capital. Rather, the brother expects to enjoy the benefits of ownership. These are a say in the management of the block, a 40% share in the income stream, and a 40% share in the proceeds of eventual sale. In this way, the provider of equity finance may be said to be an 'active' financier.

Typically, a venture capitalist will seek between 20% and 49.9% of the common shares in a company. The size of the stake must be large enough to allow the venture capitalist to influence his fellow shareholders (in particular the entrepreneur manager) while not so large as to lose sight of the fact that venture capitalists are investors not operators. Majority control is rarely sought. The shares exchanged in return for the financial injection allow the venture capitalist to share in the company's profits, to exercise voting rights in matters relating to the company's management and strategy, and to exercise all of the other rights and privileges that a co-owner or partner might enjoy.

Similar to the lender of debt capital, the equity investor must assume that his risk consists of the possibility that the venture fails so that the entire investment is lost. For the lender, however, this risk is mitigated in a number of ways. Firstly, even as an unsecured creditor the lender stands in precedence of equity investors when claims upon the company's assets are made. Secondly, the creditor will take prior claim over specific assets belonging to the company, in the form of security.

Thus, while the equity and debt investor may provide identical amounts of capital to the same recipient, the equity investor is said to incur the greater risk. The probability of success or failure of the venture will be virtually identical regardless of the form of finance provided. However, the equity investor will be less certain of its outcome, and will face a wider range of potential returns on investment than the creditor.

As an equity based form of finance, venture capital will be expected to bring the investor a higher yield than debt. In return for this desired higher yield the investor will be expected to take a greater investment risk, and back his capital injection with advice and other forms of *value added*. Like the homeowner's brother, the venture capitalist will not wish to become involved in the day-to-day running of the company. However, he will expect to share in the flow of income, to be consulted (as a partner) on major issues of policy or strategy, and to share in the proceeds of the eventual sale.

We will return to the venture capitalists' desire for superior yield, and to the nature of the investor's value added in later chapters. For the present, we turn our attention to venture capital as a form of (equity) finance.

Venture capital and its providers

First, who are the providers of venture capital? The majority (79%) of venture capital in the UK comes from the traditional sources of corporate finance, such as the high street clearing banks, the major insurance companies, pension funds, and investment management companies. (Refer to Table 1.1, below.)

For these organisations, venture capital investment is a return driven financing activity. The role of venture capital is to plug a gap in the organisation's product line or its investment portfolio. Venture capital investment activities supplement their range of corporate financial products, without which they might feel themselves at a competitive disadvantage.

Equity investing requires autonomous decision making structures

We have seen that debt lending and equity investing are not synonymous terms nor are they similar activities. Venture capital investing requires a

Capital Source	1982	1986
UK Pension Funds	27%	41%
UK Insurance Companies	7	15
Foreign Institutions	17	12
UK Banks	16	6
Fund Management Groups	na	5
SUB-TOTAL: Financial Sector	67%	79%
Private Individuals	11	15
Industrial Corporations	na	4
Others	22	2
SUB-TOTAL: Non Financial Sector	33%	21%

Table 1.1   *Sources of publicly raised venture capital in the UK – 1982 and 1986*
(Figures from Venture Economics)

different set of risks and rewards, and an investor must not assume that debt management systems, or established credit evaluation criteria can be transferred to venture capital investing activities.

The differing risks and rewards of equity compared to debt finance lead many venture capitalists to draw great distinction between their own activities and those of other corporate financiers. In the field of venture capital investment failure is an accepted – and inevitable – conclusion to certain investments, and forms one of the risks assumed in order to gain higher returns.

The traditional vetting procedures of credit finance is not necessarily appropriate to a venture capital investment. Venture portfolio companies quite often lack the traditional prerequisites to lending: a track record, a strong balance sheet, and the provision of collateral security. Greater reliance must be placed upon the quality of management, the capacity for earnings growth, and the expected value of the equity upon realisation of the investment.

The theme of differing ethos is constantly raised by venture capitalists. They highlight the need for the venture capital investment arm of a financial institution to establish and maintain a separate entity from the mainstream margin lending activities of their organisation. Autonomy is needed to allow the venture capital arm adequate scope to make long-term investment decisions without the normal credit standards and without the established relationships enjoyed by a lender.

Venture capital requires hands-on management

In light of a growing awareness of venture capital financing by entrepreneurs, small businesses and the general public in the UK, it is important to stress that venture capital is not necessarily or of itself a panacea for unemployment and does not in itself create jobs, encourage entrepreneurship, or stimulate research and development. Rather, the majority of venture investment in the UK is directed towards existing, profit making, or soon-to-be-profit making, businesses.

It would nonetheless be incorrect to view venture capital investing merely as the injection of equity capital into identified growth businesses. Venture capital investment is characterised by its hands-on, as opposed to arms-length, nature. The distinguishing features of hands-on investment are the time and effort which the investor is prepared to put into each transaction, and the after-management of each investee company within the portfolio.

As mentioned earlier, the venture capitalist will typically take between 20% and 49.9% of a company's voting equity. In some cases this will mean that the venture capital firm will be the minority shareholder, behind the entrepreneur's controlling stake. Equally likely, however, the venture capital firm's holding will make it the largest individual shareholder where two or more entrepreneurs, other investors such as employees and non-Executive Directors, or even another venture capital firm has taken equity in a company. The venture capital portfolio manager cannot therefore be content to receive a regular flow of information from his client firm, but must become personally involved in the firm's activities.

This represents a significant departure from traditional banking/lending portfolio management. One Canadian venture capitalist, with ten years' experience, has likened himself to a school teacher who had seen an entire generation of students; while a venture capitalist is not himself an entrepreneur, he has seen all kinds of businesses and business problems, and can bring that personal experience to bear.

Active portfolio management is not without its risks. Primarily, there is the risk of conflict of interest. This risk is discussed, and options for minimising the risk are considered.

Rationale for providing hands-on management

Four reasons can be given for active, participatory portfolio management.

- *Venture capital investments tend to be highly illiquid.* Unlike many other forms of finance, equity investments in unincorporated ventures generally cannot be sold on a secondary market, and losses cut. Thus, the equity investor is faced both with a long-term investment and an investment from which there exists no ready means of exit.

- *Short-term downturns in small companies with large capital requirements can have terminal results.* Even in the event of turnaround or recovery, it is unlikely that positive returns will be realised before a number of years. Therefore, when a venture capital financing is made, the investor may often find a very real need to take an active, long-term role in managing its investment.

- *Many small businesses are founded by entrepreneurs and tech-nologists.* These owner-managers often lack either the skills or the inclination to manage a growth company. Frequently, the deficiency lies in the area of financial management and control. The venture capital manager must therefore be prepared to complement the existing management team, or identify likely candidates who can. (Refer to the discussion entitled 'The Provision of Advice' in Chapter 11.)

- *The investee company expects and wants it.* In return for surrendering a portion of his equity, the entrepreneur will be seeking benefits beyond those normally supplied by a more passive investor such as a bank. The provision of expertise and advice will often be one of the key reasons that the entrepreneur will seek equity as opposed to debt capital. (A full discussion of this issue appears in Chapter 11, entitled 'What Entrepreneurs Expect From Venture Capitalists'.)

If so-called *hands-on* management is desirable, then how does it typically manifest itself? Traditionally, the venture capital firm will acquire some decision-making power, in the form of representation on the investee's Board of Directors. As one City-based venture capitalist stated:

> 'We feel that our policy of Board representation gives us a strong marketing plus.'

The 1987 survey *Venture Capital in Europe* conducted by Peat Marwick McLintock, identified 147 sources of venture capital investment in the UK. Of these, more than half stated they always required a seat on the investee company's Board of Directors, and a further quarter indicated that they usually did. (See Figure 1.1.)

Skills required for active venture capital portfolio management

Marketing, operations, strategic or technical back-up, as well as financial back-up, will often be necessary for the investment to be realised. Alan Patricof, Managing Director of Alan Patricof Associates, an international venture capital company, made the following comments to a symposium of European venture capitalists, on the subject of

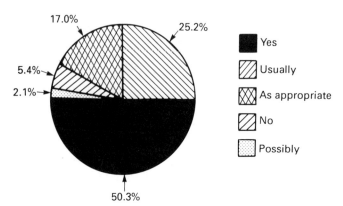

Figure 1.1 Directorship requirements of UK venture investment firms. (Figures from Peat Marwick McLintock)

recruiting and training venture capitalists:

'Surprisingly, financial skills are not as essential a talent as would initially seem to be the case. Although the understanding of balance sheets and income statements and the way in which profits are developed are necessary, I would not place this as the paramount skill necessary.'

What was crucial, in Patricof's opinion, were 'people skills':

'People skills are crucial. Venture capitalists by their nature tend to be egotists and the entrepreneurs they are backing are also egotists, and because the venture capitalist controls the availability of capital there is a built-in dependence which the entrepreneur is never quite happy with. It is essential for a venture capitalist to have the personality to inspire an entrepreneur, to be supportive and at the same time to provide dispassionate outside advice and, in some cases, to make decisions which are not always favourably received. Nevertheless, this kind of relationship which involves mutual respect is a prerequisite to a successful team effort. For this reason it is important that the venture capitalist has enough experience to command that type of respect from the outset.' (*Source: Improving Venture Capital Opportunities in Europe*, Commission of the European Communities, Brussels, 1985.)

This opinion was affirmed by other British venture capitalists who, in discussions with the author, also considered people skills and *personal chemistry* as the key to making a venture capital investment into a successful business relationship, and by extension, into a financial success.

While difficult to define in precise terms, personal chemistry can be described as excellent interpersonal skills, combined with an entre- preneurial – as opposed to a purely financial – management orientation. Many venture capitalists rate personal satisfaction, and the opportunity to assist in the management of the investee company as the prime motivators to their activities. In this respect, the successful venture capital investor shares a common motivation with the entrepreneur.

Next to these people skills and personal chemistry the venture capital portfolio manager needs good general management skills – as opposed to purely financial skills. The view is widely held that the ability to provide general management advice (i.e. a balanced view of finance, marketing, production and strategy, etc.) is one of the primary means by which the venture capitalist adds value to his portfolio. To some firms, this has meant a preference for hiring venture capital executives possessing technical or line management experience in lieu of those with accounting or banking backgrounds.

These points have implications on the attributes of the successful venture capital executive. Previous line management would appear to be a strong asset. A long track record in industry, or previous experience as a venture capitalist would give the venture capital manager credibility. Finally, entrepreneurial flair is as important as financial expertise.

Benefits of hands-on venture capital portfolio management

Advocates of the hands-on approach point to a series of value added effects from active portfolio management. For the investee hands-on management by the investor has the following advantages:

- Hands-on management is more than merely active, it is pro-active, i.e. the active investor may anticipate difficulties and take steps to avoid them, as opposed to merely reading about them in a quarterly report.

- The venture capitalist, being at least skilled in investment and finance, can often bring expertise to the investor in these areas.

- The venture capitalist can, through his contacts in the world of finance and investment, often find additional sources of capital in the event that turn-around or bridge financing may be required when an investee company develops liquidity problems. The majority of entrepreneurs indicate a desire for such assistance. (Refer to the discussion of 'The Provision of Second Round Finance' in Chapter 11.)

Risks of hands-on involvement

Not all practising venture investors agree as to the merits of hands-on investment management. Active, hands-on portfolio management is not without its risks.

Some practitioners maintain that 'hands-on' portfolio managers are at best deluding, and at worst flattering themselves. Those who reject hands-on portfolio management maintain that the professional venture capital executive, with a responsibility to maintain a deal flow, and perform 'due diligence' in evaluating current proposals, has not the time nor sufficient knowledge of each investee to bring any real value added.

Many hands-off venture capital managers have expressed concern about the Insolvency and Directors Liability Act (1986) with its provisions for increasing the personal liability of Company Directors in the case of a business failure. Some venture capital managers have expressed concern about the prospect of personal liability, and the potential for conflicts of interest which the active venture capital manager encounters. The question arises: To whom does the venture capital manager owe his first loyalty, the investor whose funds he is managing or the investee on whose Board he may sit?

To address this risk of conflicting interests, some financial institutions have adopted a policy of being both sole lender and sole investor in instances where they are supplying both debt and equity to the investee. This mitigates the risk of having a conflict of interest, and the risk of legal action where other lenders or investors may feel their interests have been jeopardised.

To avoid the appearance of conflict of interest, many venture capital firms practise what might be called the 'hands-hovering' style of portfolio management. Here, the investor reserves the right, seldom exercised, to take a position on the Board of the investee company. The key to hands-hovering portfolio management is to be not so active so as to jeopardise the independence of the entrepreneur, and not so arm's length as to undermine his confidence.

The key appears to be not so much a commitment to either 'hands-on' or 'hands-off' management a priori, rather, the venture capitalist should be in a position to bring assistance quickly and directly when needed, while knowing when to leave well enough alone. If implemented and operated effectively, hands-on management can have at worst a neutral, at best a very positive effect. Often the value added brought by the venture capitalist may come in subtle or unanticipated forms. Contacts, certainly, may be one of the most important and sometimes unanticipated results of having an active equity investor. Other benefits are more obvious, financial, general management or strategic advice, as well as access to legal and other expertise.

3

Superior returns through capital gain

Given the risks inherent in providing equity as opposed to debt, it follows that those in the business of providing venture capital must do so only if the expected value of their return on investment is sufficiently high to justify those risks. Debt financiers, such as banks, whose range of possible returns can be narrowed, can lend to borrowers promising only moderate returns. The venture capitalist must offset his risk by confining his investments to ventures exhibiting potential for above average returns on equity. The figure normally cited is for a return of approximately 40% per annum, compounded. Phrased differently, many venture capitalists refer to 'a three times return after three years' or 'a five times return after five years'.

In seeking individual investments with above average returns, the vast majority of venture capital firms accept that some proportion of their portfolio will in fact yield only a marginal or no return at all. Most of the venture capital investors surveyed during the course of writing this book readily conceded that two out of ten venture capital investments will fail altogether. A further six investments out of ten, the bulk of the venture capital investment portfolio, are expected to yield no more than the market rate of return. These will provide a steady, but unremarkable income which will sustain the portfolio. Only two investments in ten are expected to yield the extraordinary returns which will raise the overall return of the portfolio. This phenomenon is known in the industry as the rule of $2:6:2$, indicating the relative occurrence of outright losers, acceptable investments and clear winners in any venture capital portfolio.

In becoming an equity investor, the venture capital firm exposes itself to the widest possible range of returns. This is the nature of the venture capitalist's *risk*: not a lower expected return but a greater, and less certain range of returns.

In this chapter we look at the return on investment typically sought by providers of venture capital finance in the UK. These figures are based to a large extent on empirical evidence as to rates of return experienced by the venture capital industries in the United States and Canada, and to a lesser extent by venture capital firms in the UK.

We will also consider factors which affect return on investment performance and the high degree of discrimination and the low conversion rates of most venture capitalists when reviewing business plans.

Level of ROI sought by venture capital investors

It was stated above that the venture capital investor seeks to realise a three times return after three years or a five times return after five years, or roughly 40% per annum. These return on investment targets are merely convenient shorthand, since most venture capitalists in fact alter their hurdle rate depending upon the nature of the investment, and the degree of management time and effort that will be involved to bring the investment to fruition. Generally speaking, the more advanced the company is in its development, the lower the rate of return the venture capital investors will require.

Empirical evidence

Hard data on actual rates of return for private venture capital firms within the UK industry are difficult to obtain. This is in the first place because the majority of venture capital firms are private companies. Financial statements are not readily made available. Furthermore, most venture capital firms are less than five years old. For those investing in all but the latest stages of company development, the full investment portfolio has not yet matured. Also, the profitability which a venture capital firm realises comes from capital gain, not current income. Therefore, much of a venture capital firm's future profitability will be represented by investments carried on its balance sheets at its historic cost, not its current value.

Among UK publicly quoted venture capital companies with a fully

IRR % Reported	Number of Firms Reporting	Percentage of Firms Reporting
< than 10%	3	7
10 to 20%	5	11
21 to 40%	18	39
41 to 100%	7	15
> than 100%	3	7
no answer/don't know	10	21
TOTAL	46	100

Table 1.2   *Internal rates of return for a sample of 46 US venture capital firms*
(Figures from Tyebjee and Bruno)

matured portfolio, Equity Capital for Industry (ECI) reports in its annual report of 1987 an overall annual rate of return of 30%. In their annual report 3i state a five year average ROI, to the end of 1988, of more than 22%. This figure does not breakout the returns from its venture capital as opposed to its margin lending activities.

Other UK venture capital firms have verbally reported the following:

• 40% internal rate of return is reasonably conservative.

• On target to the desired ROI of 30% per annum.

• Estimated 40% per annum return on investment.

Actual rates of return to be realised from venture investing can be taken from the US experience, with its long history and its large sample size of both publicly owned and private venture capital firms. A 1983 American study of 46 US venture capital firms found that most venture capital firms realised yields of between 21% and 40% and that fully three-fifths enjoyed returns in excess of 20% per annum. (Refer to Table 1.2.)

Factors affecting ROI performance

Returns reported by venture capitalists in North America and the United Kingdom typically range between 30–40% per year, compounded. These figures may be subject to hard scrutiny because for many UK venture firms these are still early years. In addition, many venture capital portfolios, particularly those with a technology focus, were adversely affected by the generally poor performance of the electronics and technology sectors in the mid-1980s.

Nevertheless, most venture capitalists in the UK are confident that returns in the range of 20% to 30% per annum may be attainable through:

- fundamental analysis;

- financial analysis, including sensitivity;

- portfolio diversification;

- appropriate operational controls;

- the recruitment of qualified management personnel;

- a little good fortune.

Experience indicates that venture capital managers are highly discriminating in their portfolio choice. Very few unsolicited business plans proceed beyond only the most cursory stages of analysis. Research suggests that only 2% to 5% of all business plans progress to financing. (Refer to Table 1.3.)

Reasons for this low yield are many, but one appears to stand ahead of all others. Only about one in every 100 applications for venture backing is successful, mainly because of the view that management is considered to be no good.

While recognising the need to maintain constant deal flow, the industry's low conversion rate means that efficient and effective management and processing systems are essential. One means of increasing the

Bank Captive Venture Capital Company	Business Plans Reviewed Annually	Annual Investments	Investments as % of Plans
Charterhouse Dev. Capital	600	60	10
Clydesdale Bank Equity	250	5–6	2–3
Barclays Development Capital	na	na	5
Lloyds Development Capital	400	15–20	4–5

Table 1.3 *Business plans proceeding to investment – bank captive venture firms*

conversion rate of business plans to investments is for the venture capitalist to specialise. It can do so by carefully targeting its investment activities to those market niches which will include only those stages of development, industrial sectors, technological intensities and organisation types for which its managers have a proven knowledge and competence, and there is a high probability that a business plan will progress beyond only the most superfluous examination.

The most crucial determinant of venture capital portfolio yield is, clearly, choosing the right company to invest in at the outset. Only a tiny proportion of business plans reviewed by venture capitalists actually proceed to investment stage. The UK experience is for an investment rate of some 2% to 5% (see below). Venture capitalists evaluate business proposals in order to identify risks and estimate returns. Thus, essential to the screening process is an estimation of probable losses and gains. These are subjected to sensitivity analyses and expected value calculations. Only after clearing these hurdles will a company be deemed worthy of venture capital finance. Part three of this book examines, in greater detail, the factors which venture capitalists consider when making their investment analysis.

The second determinant of venture capital return will be the selection of a portfolio which is adequately diversified by geographic location, industry sector, and stage of corporate development. Enterprises in the earliest stages of their corporate development normally represent the greatest source of risk, but should, through proper management and appropriate operational controls, yield the greatest returns. Part two of this book, entitled 'Seven Stages of Venture Capital Funding' considers the various stages of venture capital investment in some depth. Chapter 23 entitled 'Patterns of Venture capital Investment' considers recent trends in venture capital investment by geographic location and by industry sector.

Venture capital requires patience

Ultimately, the reward from venture capital investing come when the venture capitalist sells his shares to another buyer. Typically the payoff will come through one of four means of realisation or *exit*:

- Trade Sale
- Earn Out

- Take Out
- Flotation

These divestment mechanisms will be considered in greater detail in Chapter 11, 'Analysing Venture Capital Proposals'.

Whichever is the eventual exit mechanism, the prospective venture capital investor must be prepared to recognise that none of them will come quickly. Venture capital investments take a long time to mature. Given their focus on sometimes small, usually unlisted firms, venture capital investments lack the liquidity of an investment in a listed firm. The industry tends also to be cyclical, its fortunes fluctuating with the initial placement market. These factors highlight the need for patience.

In establishing an illiquid, long-term portfolio, an investor must recognise two prerequisites. One, which lies within the control of the portfolio manager, is the need for patience. The second, which lies outside the control of the portfolio manager, is the need for a political economy that is sympathetic and conducive toward long-term equity investment.

The rationale for patience

Venture capital is long-term finance. The industry norm appears to be to look for an investment with a three to five year return, although six to ten years to realisation is quite within the spectrum of venture capital portfolio investment. A 1987 *Survey of the Impact of Venture Capital* in the UK comprising 92 UK firms which had been financed by venture capital and then gone public, and conducted by the accounting firm Arthur Andersen on behalf of the British Venture Capital Association indicated that the average venture investment was realised in 3.5 years. As previously noted, a similar survey in Canada indicated that venture investments tend to be realised after 4.1 years.

One observation gained from the interviews with practising venture capitalists in both the UK and North America is that the venture capitalist will talk to the investee in terms of a two to five year investment horizon, while being prepared to live with investments with a maturity of two to three years longer than that. Three reasons can be given for these different perspectives:

- Venture capital investment is a highly cyclical activity. Exits are necessarily a function of the receptivity of the public equity markets for initial placement offerings (IPOs), and a function of the price-to-earnings multiples (P : Es) being offered in the market place. If these latter are experiencing their cyclical low, the venture capitalist and entrepreneur alike may see advantage in delaying a public offering.

- It is not unusual for the value of a venture capital company to decrease by some 20% to 25% in the first three or four years of its operation.

- It is a well-known phenomenon within the industry that winners take longer to surface than losers. Bad investments are observed to surface within the first twelve months after the investment is made. Winners, on the other hand may take up to five years to yield the returns normally sought by a venture equity investor.

In general terms it can be said that the venture capital industry represents a balance between risk and return. The risks arise early while the returns require patience and perseverance.

The role of political stability

Political stability is normally an essential necessary condition for successful long term investment. This pre-condition was largely absent from the UK investment environment during the 1960s and the early 1970s, and its absence was noted both by the Wilson Committee and, at various times, by the Bank of England.

Of equal importance is a sympathetic fiscal environment. Taxation rates on business income and capital investment must, in the ideal, be low and at very least be stable, so that expected returns can be calculated with some degree of confidence.

During the past decade, a number of factors have contributed to an improved climate for long term equity investment. Generally, ten years of a government with generally free-market, and entrepreneurial attitudes and policies have provided a suitable backcloth. Specifically, the following dimensions of policy are noted:

- *Falling Inflation.* Retail price inflation has fallen from more than 20% at its peak in 1980 to 4% in 1987. This had risen to 8 or 9% by mid-1989, its highest level since 1982, an upward trend which no doubt weakened business confidence somewhat.

- *Economic Growth.* In real terms, the economy has grown at an average rate of 3¼% per year since 1983.

- *Falling Personal Tax Rates.* The basic rate of tax on personal income has seen three successive reductions, from 30% to 25%. Equally, the top marginal rate of tax has fallen from more than 80% to 40%. Falling personal income tax rates have caused a spurt in personal sector savings, a significant contributor to the pool of venture capital.

- *Falling Small Business Corporation Tax.* The rate of tax on small business has followed the basic rate of personal tax from 30% to 25%.

- *Business Expansion Scheme.* The introduction of the BES in 1983 created an entire new, tax assisted pool of venture capital funding. Subsequent budgets have expanded the scope of the BES, including the budget of 1988 which allowed greater latitude for investing in real estate related companies.

It is essential that venture investors recognise the illiquid and long term nature of their portfolio. This point is continually stressed by practising venture capitalists.

Irrespective of one's political stripe, it must be accepted that a political and economic climate characterised by a majority government and declining personal and corporate taxes, are conducive to the provision of venture capital investment and the receptivity of entrepreneurs to this form of finance.

4

Summary

In this part of the book, the reader has gained an operational knowledge of the term 'venture capital'. The intent was to focus on the key strategy and management issues involved in venture capital investment. Its key features provided on page 4, are restated here for the sake of clarity. Venture capital:

- Is equity finance.

- Requires hands-on management.

- Provides superior return through capital gain.

- Requires patience.

First, venture capital is identified as *Equity finance*. As such, it stands as an alternative or complement to other forms of corporate finance which a financial institution may provide or which an entrepreneur may seek. It was noted that:

- The current providers of venture capital in the UK are, in the main (79%), the traditional providers of corporate finance: the banks, the pension funds, and the insurance companies.

- The risk involved in equity investment differs from that of debt finance, primarily in that it offers a greater, and less certain, range of returns.

- Unlike traditional bank lending, venture capital investing presupposes that a significant proportion of the investments will fail. The percentage of unsuccessful investments normally cited is 20%.

- To protect their separate ethos, the venture capital arm must function independent of the lending institution and this separation should be protected through erecting 'Chinese Walls'.

- The traditional vetting procedures of credit finance may not necessarily be appropriate to an equity investment. Entrepreneurial companies may often lack the traditional prerequisites to bank lending: a track record, a strong balance sheet, and the provision of collateral security. Greater reliance must be placed upon the quality of management, the capacity for earnings growth, and the expected value of the equity upon realisation of the investment.

Second, venture capital *requires hands-on management*. The following rationale was noted:

- Venture capital investments tend to be highly illiquid;

- Venture capital investments are long term to fruition;

- Entrepreneurs want it;

- Investee firms may need it.

This has implications as to the qualities of venture capital executives:

- Venture capitalists stressed the need for good personal chemistry between investor and investee. Some likened venture investing to a marriage. Others stressed the need for the venture capitalist to inspire the confidence of his investee.

- General management as well as purely financial skills are required of the venture capital manager.

- Those skills can best be brought to bear at Board level. Active Board participation is seen as essential to monitoring the investment, and giving the venture capitalist the opportunity to supply value added finance, without being so hands-on as to stifle the entrepreneur/manager or his independence.

Hands-on investment may entail certain risks. The particular risk noted was the possibility of conflicts of interest arising. Appropriate control and administrative procedures must be established so as to minimise these.

Third, venture capital investment *provides superior return through capital gain*. The following issues with respect to returns were noted:

- Providers of venture capital investment are highly selective in their choice of ventures to fund.
- The empirical evidence from North America suggests that returns on investment average 20% to 30% per annum.
- Most UK venture capital firms claim 30% per annum as their actual or target return on investment.
- Venture capitalists seek superior returns on any given investment, with 40% normally being seen as the minimum acceptable hurdle rate.
- Winners take time to surface, and patience is required if the portfolio is to yield the returns anticipated.
- With time, good portfolio management, and luck, the empirical evidence indicates that a portfolio return of 20% to 30% per annum is attainable.

Fourth, venture capital investment *requires patience*. Recent evidence regarding realisations show that average term to fruition in the United Kingdom is 3.5 years, whereas in North America it tends to be longer. Patience is required for four reasons:

- The industry is cyclical, and is tied to the vagaries of the public listed exchanges in terms of receptiveness to initial placements and flotations.
- Experience indicates that the value of a venture capital portfolio will fall before it climbs.
- 'Winners' will take longer to realise than 'losers'.
- The success of any long term investment is inevitably tied to the political and economic climate, particularly as it might impact on small or emerging business.

Part two

Seven stages of venture capital funding

5

Seven stages of venture capital funding: introduction

In the introduction to venture capital finance, it was inferred that venture capital investment is a homogeneous product; i.e. all long term equity investments made by professional investors are made in the same kinds of companies, for the same kinds of reasons, and with the same sorts of expectations concerning risk, maturity, and investment performance. This is obviously not the case.

In the lending arena, we can distinguish between a large variety of loan products, for example, overdrafts (to cover the household bills on a monthly basis), car loans (which might have a maturity of 3 to 5 years), and home mortgages (which have a maturity of 25 years). Because different varieties of loans involve different sets of risks, rewards and expectations, lending institutions sometimes specialise in different products, or become the dominant suppliers of these products. While the distinctions between banks and building societies are rapidly becoming blurred, it is a matter of tradition that UK consumers typically maintained their overdraft with the former, while obtaining their mortgage from the latter.

The situation is similar for the supply of venture capital. Broadly speaking, various strategies and approaches to venture capital funding can be distinguished by the stage of the investee company's life and the time – and therefore the risk – associated with bringing an investee company to maturity. Different venture capital firms will have differing aptitudes and appetites for various kinds of venture capital investment. The purpose of this part of the book is to provide a framework for identifying and differentiating between different types of venture capital.

The various stages of the venture capital life cycle provide such a framework. By identifying various stages in the life cycle of a typical company, we can identify the different types of venture capital investment appropriate at an individual stage. Niches for each venture capitalist's capabilities and its desired risk/reward profile will be identified.

Note that in Part one venture capital investment did not restrict itself to firms which are necessarily small or firms which are necessarily young. Rather (as will be discussed at greater length in Part four) UK venture capital investment flows into companies at all stages of development.

We can identify seven different stages of venture capital investing. However, few companies, if any, will require external funding at each of the seven stages described. Certainly, few suppliers of venture capital will be able to provide for them all. In many investments the distinction between one stage of investee development and another will be blurred. (When does a company pass through its start-up and into its early growth stage?) Some firms may achieve flotation on a junior stock market prior to reaching full maturity. Some owner-managers may reach their *comfort level* while the firm is still growing. Some companies, quite simply, will fail.

The stages of the venture capital life cycle are examined in the approximate order in which an investee company would require each form of finance. They range from an investment type which may take eight years or longer for realisation (seed capital) to one which, by its very nature, is intended purely as bridge finance (mezzanine). The venture capital life cycle can be described as consisting of the following stages:

- Seed capital

- Start-up capital

- Early stage finance

- Second round finance

- Expansion capital

- Management buy-outs and buy-ins

- Mezzanine finance

Successive chapters discuss aspects of each stage of the life cycle. The discussion of each stage considers:

- a working definition;
- the characteristics of a typical investee company;
- the approximate term to realisation of the investment;
- recent statistics on volumes of investment activity;
- the principal features and risks of each.

Part two ends with a general set of conclusions concerning the 'Seven Stages of Venture Capital Funding'.

The venture capital life cycle

Graphically, the venture capital life cycle can be depicted by the model illustrated in Figure 2.1 below:

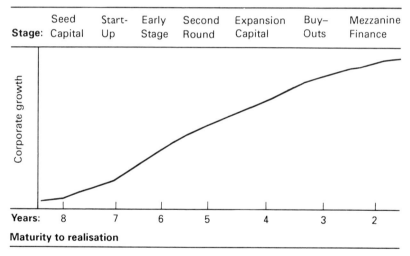

Figure 2.1 The venture capital life cycle – stages of unquoted equity investment.

The horizontal axis depicts the approximate maturity to realisation for each type of investment. Typically, realisation will occur when the investee firm has reached a level of maturity such that it can go public via a share flotation on the Unlisted Securities Market. Alternatively, it may become an attractive candidate for acquisition by a larger firm. The vertical axis depicts the company's growth. This growth may be by whatever measure the investor may prefer to use: growth in assets, in turnover or in earnings. Beginning at the bottom left hand corner of the diagram, a firm will have yet to realise much growth and be many years away from the size or maturity where it can go public. As time passes, a successful firm would move diagonally upward and to the right, growing and coming closer to maturity. Note that the growth curve slows, and arrives in the top right hand corner as an established, maturing firm displaying steady growth.

6

Seed capital and start-up capital

Seed capital

The rationale for providing seed capital investment is that from tiny acorns mighty oak trees grow. Seed capital is investment into the gem of an idea, or a concept – as opposed to a business.

Definition

The European Venture Capital Association defines seed capital as:

> The financing of the initial product development or the capital provided to an entrepreneur to prove the feasibility of a project and qualify for start-up capital. (P. De Vree, quoted in Proceedings of the EVCI No. 1, 1988.)

Characteristics

The characteristics of a seed corn investment might be:

- the absence of a ready to market product;

- the absence of a complete management team;

- a product or process which is still in the research or development stage.

Typically, seed corn enterprises lack the asset base and/or the track record to obtain debt from conventional sources (working capital lines or bank term loans) and are largely dependent upon the entrepreneur's personal resources.

Term to realisation
Broadly speaking, a seed capital investment may take from 7 to 10 years to achieve realisation.

Seed capital: volume of investment activity

In the UK the majority of venture funds other than certain specialists seldom make seed capital investments, and these are relatively small by comparison to other forms of venture finance. Seed corn finance represented less than 1% of the value of venture capital invested in the United Kingdom in 1988. (Refer to Table 2.1.)

The absence of an interest in providing a significant amount of seed capital can be attributed to four main factors:

- *Seed capital projects, by their very nature, require a relatively small amount of capital.* The success or failure of an individual seed capital investment will have very little impact on the performance of all but the smallest venture capitalist's portfolio. Larger venture capital firms will therefore avoid seed capital investments if these will have little impact on the investor's balance sheet, or place disproportionate demands on its human resources.

- *Small investments are not seen to be cost efficient* in terms of the man-hours required to analyse, structure and manage them. Venture capital managers stress that a small investment takes as much work as a large one, rendering seed capital projects inefficient in terms of cost to administer.

Year	Seed Capital Investments	Seed as % of Total	Seed Capital Invested	Seed as % of Total	Average Seed Investment
1988	13	0.6	£1.1m	0.1	£85,615
1987	n.a.	n.a.	£1.9m	0.1	n.a.

Table 2.1 *Seed capital as proportion of total UK venture finance – 1987 and 1988 (Figures from Peat Marwick McLintock and the EVCA)*

- *The time horizon to realisation* for most seed-corn investments (typically 7 to 10 years) is longer than all but the most long-term oriented investors will desire.

- *The risk of product and technology obsolescence increases* as the time to realisation is extended. These types of obsolescence may be particularly likely to occur with high-technology type investments.

Seed capital: features and risks

Seed capital financing has the distinction of being the earliest, and therefore the riskiest stage of venture capital investment. To compensate for these risks, venture capitalists apply higher discount rates to early stage investments than for the shorter maturity, less risky, later stage financings. The Scottish Development Agency for example, has been reported to require a 50% rate of return on seed capital investments.

However, while the earliest stages of financing are those fraught with the highest risk, they also provide the greatest opportunity for acquiring a bargain. At the seed capital stage, the entrepreneur himself may not know precisely what he has to offer. He is less able to negotiate generous terms for his existing equity. At the earliest stages of a company's life, perhaps even before the business concept has evolved into a corporate body, the entrepreneur will be looking for more than just cash, and will have to surrender a greater proportion of his equity in return for a greater degree of support and assistance (in the form of product development, planning or marketing advice) supplied by the venture capital investor. It is these earliest stage investments which provide the greatest potential for realising significant capital gains in the long term.

Practising venture capitalists advise that they are less willing to provide these earliest stages of finance. The asset underlying the investment at the seed capital stage is often a technology or an idea, as opposed to the human assets (good managers) so often sought by venture capital investors. As such, this approach to seed capital funding may be in violation of one of the cardinal rules of venture capital investment, that ventures should be evaluated on the strength of the three Ms: Management, Management, and Management.

Recent American research examined the rate of return actually achieved on venture capital invested in 50 firms in the United States. Three characteristics were significantly related to the rates of return achieved by the investor. The stage of development and the extensiveness of market evaluation were positively related. The proportion of equity owned by the venture capitalist was negatively related. Thus, chances of higher return are improved by investing in ventures where product development and market assessment are complete and the entrepreneur holds a large stake in the equity. This would seem to weigh against investing in seed capital projects, where product development and market assessment will not have been completed, and where the entrepreneur is unlikely to have sufficient financial resources so as to retain a high percentage of the equity.

It is at the seed capital stage, however, that an active venture investor with a general management approach, may be able to provide the greatest 'value-added' to his investment. He can do this by providing financial skills or using his contacts to introduce production, marketing, strategic, or general management skills to the investment.

The seed capital providers

On a more practical level, seed capital investment may pose certain problems to those who are lured by the prospects of its high anticipated returns. Given that most venture capital funds are reluctant or unwilling to provide seed capital finance, the risk seeking venture capitalist will find himself in a sole investor or, at best, in a lead investor position. Syndications will be difficult, as will the ability to attract outside funds for second round or take-out financing. Once invested, the highly illiquid nature of seed capital financing means that the venture capitalist is committed.

The most notable player in the seed capital business is British Technologies Group (BTG). With £62 million of funds under management BTG is the principal supplier of (technology oriented) seed and start-up funding in the UK. BTG is not an equity investor in the usual mould of venture providers, taking ordinary voting equity only in unusual cases. It is, however, a provider of equity-type (interest free, income related) capital.

BTG is one of the few UK venture capital firms which will invest in the somewhat esoteric field of intellectual property rights (IPR). Here the investment is made not into a company but into a specific product or technology within a company. The investor receives its return through a percentage of the product purchase or a licence fee/royalty stream. In legal terms IPR investments are little different from equity investments, although they may be very time consuming. IPR investments may require extensive and costly product development before they can be realised.

Seed capital: conclusions

The principal conclusion drawn is that while opportunities for profitable seed capital investing may exist, in practice venture capitalists tend to apply high discount rates against investment proposals at this stage.

Individual seed capital investments tend to involve relatively small amounts of capital, and therefore, may not be suitable for firms with larger pools of funds or limited management resources.

The attributes required for successful seed capital investing would appear to be:

- project management skills;

- a degree of technical competence on the part of the investor;

- a very long (perhaps seven to ten years) investment horizon;

- an ability of the venture capitalist to work with scientists and technologists as opposed to managers.

The time to analyse, time to realisation and the risks inherent in seed capital investment make it unattractive to the majority of venture capital firms.

Start-up capital

Start-up capital is the second stage in the venture capital cycle and is distinguishable from seed capital investment in that the investee has moved closer toward the establishment of a going concern. The business concept has been fully investigated, and the business risk now becomes that of turning the concept into a product.

Definition
The European Venture Capital Association (EVCA) defines start-up capital as:

> Capital needed to finance the product development, initial marketing and the establishment of product facilities. (P. De Vree, as quoted in the Proceedings of EVCI, No. 1, 1988.)

Characteristics
The characteristics of a start-up venture will typically be:

- the establishment of a company, whether by incorporation or partnership;

- the establishment of some – but not all – of the management team;

- the development of a business plan, and a prototype product or fully developed idea;

- the absence of a trading record.

Term to realisation
The time horizon for a start-up investment will typically be some 6 to 8 years. The study mentioned on p. 21 indicated that, of 92 firms surveyed, 10% had received start-up capital and had taken an average of 8.25 years to reach public flotation.

Start-up capital: volume of investment activity

Despite the potential for spectacular returns from winners, most UK venture firms avoid investing in start-ups. In 1988, less than 15% of venture capital investments, representing 5.3% by value, went to start-ups. (Refer to Table 2.2.)

One reason for the paucity of start-up financings may be the high discount rates that venture capitalists apply to venture proposals of this level of risk and maturity. One well established venture capital firm uses a 50–100% hurdle rate in evaluating start-ups.

Year	Start-Up Capital Investments	Start-Up as % of Total	Start-Up Capital Invested	Start-Up as % of Total	Average Start-Up Investment
1988	202	14.8	£70.0	5.3	£346,500
1987	191	15.8	£75.1	8.0	£393,200
1986	113	17.8	£57.9m	15.1	£512,400
1985	92	16.9	£31.6m	11.7	£343,500

Table 2.2 *Start-up capital as proportion of total UK venture finance – 1985 to 1988 (Figures from the BVCA)*

Peat Marwick's 1987 study *Major Sources for Venture Capital in the UK* revealed that 91 of the 147 firms identified (62%) claim to provide start-up capital. However, this research suggests that many firms who fund start-ups in theory shun them in practice. This may be because of the large size of many venture capitalists' balance sheets, and the diseconomies of effort applied to smaller proposals, rather than for reasons of fundamental risk.

Start-up capital: features and risks

With a start-up proposition the venture capitalist's investment criteria shifts from the idea behind the company to the people behind the company and the market opportunity represented by the management's realisation of the idea. Venture capital for start-up situations tends to be more along the classic lines of American venture capital, with its emphasis on backing entrepreneurs as opposed to companies. The number of UK venture capital firms willing to invest in start-up situations is still relatively small.

3i is one firm which, because of its long track record, its ability to take a long term position, and its relative sophistication, is willing to invest in start-up situations. Other likely sources of start-up capital are the government backed venture capital providers.

Start-up capital: conclusions

It appears that the start-up capital investment engenders less risk to the venture capitalist than does seed capital investment. However, the term to realisation for the typical start-up investment (empirically 8.25 years) remains dramatically longer than the term of finance normally provided by the majority of financial institutions.

Somewhat more than half of UK venture capital firms indicate a willingness to provide start-up capital, suggesting a greater number of syndication opportunities and possibly some take-outs. In practice it appears nevertheless that the majority in fact shun this stage of investment.

7

Early stage finance, second round finance and expansion capital

Early stage finance

As a company matures, it becomes a less risky investment for the would-be provider of equity capital. As it passes through the start-up and into the early success stage of its life cycle, a proven management team will have been put into place, a range of products will have been established and an identifiable market will have been targeted.

Definition

The British Venture Capital Association defines an early stage finance as:

> Finance provided to companies that have completed the product development stage and require further funds to initiate commercial manufacturing and sales. They will not yet be generating profit. (*Report on Investment Activity, 1986.*)

Characteristics

Characteristics of an early stage company might be:

- Little or no sales revenue.

- Cash flow and profits are still negative.

- A small but enthusiastic management team which consists in most cases of entrepreneurs with a technical or specialist background and with little experience in the management of a growing business.

- Short term prospects for dramatic revenue and profit growth.

Term to realisation

Early stage investments might typically have a four to six year time horizon to realisation.

Early stage finance: volume of investment activity

Recent BVCA statistics suggest that fewer early stage financings are made compared to start-ups (182 versus 202 in the latest year). On average, the value of early stage venture funding is less than that for start-ups (£329,700 versus £346,500). This might reflect the increased ability of the entrepreneurial firm to attract debt as opposed to equity finance. Alternatively, it might reflect the greater ability of early stage firms to generate funds internally. Nevertheless, the early stage investment is not without sufficient risks that high rates of return are sought. One Edinburgh based venture investor advised that discount rates of between 50% and 60% are his normal criterion for this stage of investment.

Early stage finance accounted for 13.4% of the investments made by the member firms of the British Venture Capital Association in 1988, representing just 4.6% by value. (Refer to Table 2.3.)

Early stage finance: features and risks

To the venture capitalist, an early stage financing is perhaps the earliest in which two of the fundamental aspects of an investible business are in place: a fully assembled management team and a marketable product. The fundamental risk has therefore changed from factors internal to the

Year	Number of Early Stage Investments	Investments as % of Total	Value of Early Stage Investments	Value as % of Total	Average Size of Investment
1988	182	13.4	£60.0m	4.6	£329,700
1987	133	11.0	£45.3m	4.9	£340,600
1986	76	12.0	£28.2m	7.3	£371,000
1985	62	11.4	£17.5m	6.5	£282,000

Table 2.3 *Early stage as proportion of total UK venture finance – 1985 to 1988* (Figures from the BVCA)

firm (lack of management, lack of product) to factors external to the firm (competitive pressures, insufficient willingness of banks to provide adequate capital, risk of product obsolescence, etc.).

Equity investment at the early growth stage is key to the survival of the entrepreneurial firm. Without the foundation of a trading record, debt finance will be difficult to obtain. Yet, it is precisely at this stage of a firm's life that its capital needs, particularly working capital needs, are greatest. Equity provides funds for fast growing firms without the associated debt burden. At the start-up stage the traditional resources may have been personal savings, and those of friends, relatives and private benefactors. Beyond that, of necessity, early stage firms become increasingly dependent on venture capitalists.

However, a number of risks inevitably remain. These may include:

- The early stage company has entered into the critical part of its development and, while business success is within reach, the firm continues to be highly susceptible to fundamental risks. This might include the defection of key personnel, in search of greater security, when management depth is thin or non-existent.

- The early stage firm may have drawn the attention of, and incurred the challenges of, a larger competitor.

- Even where the firm has developed a product with proven marketability, there remains the risk of product obsolescence. The latter will be particularly true where the firm is involved in a technology intense line of business.

Early stage finance: conclusions

The absence of either profits or a positive cash flow continue to make the early stage investment too risky for typical Clearing Bank lending. However, the existence of a product and a management team considerably reduce the fundamental risk facing the equity investor with patience.

Generally, the shorter time horizons and decreased fundamental risks associated with early stage firms make them more attractive as venture investments than either seed capital or start-up situations.

The number of venture capitalists active at this stage, as judged by recent volumes of investment activity, appears to be relatively small.

Second round finance

The would-be venture capitalist should recognise that the owner-manager is looking for a partner with a strong balance sheet, a generous supply of patience, and the willingness to ride out the inevitable set-backs. It is stressed that venture capital investing often, and as a matter of course, may call for a second and sometimes third injection of capital. (A full discussion of the expectations of entrepreneurial firms with regard to continuing finance appears in Chapter 11.) The provisional need for an investor prepared to dig into deep pockets will therefore drive many entrepreneurs to seek larger, better capitalised investors.

Definition
Second round or 'follow-on' finance can be defined as the provision of capital to a firm which has previously been in receipt of external capital but whose financial needs have subsequently expanded.

Characteristics
Typically, the firm requiring second round finance will have:

- a developed product on the market;

- a full management team in place;

- sales revenues being generated from one or more products;

- losses on the income statement or, when it is breaking even, a negative cash flow.

Term to realisation
In the venture capital life cycle, second round financing will typically come after the start-up and early stage funding, and should be expected to have a shorter term to maturity.

Second round finance: features and risks

Reasons for second round financing are many, and include both the positive and the negative. Negative reasons may include:

- cost over-runs in product development;

- the failure of new products to live up to sales forecasts;
- the need to reposition products through a new marketing campaign;
- the need to refine a flawed product once its deficiencies are revealed in the testing ground of the market place.

On the positive side, follow-on financing is sometimes called for when preliminary sales results appear to be exceeding forecast, and the firm needs to acquire assets, including people, to gear up for production volumes greater than forecast. Depending on their payment and collection policies, high growth companies sometimes expand faster than their ability to finance their working capital needs without the benefit of additional finance.

Provision for additional finance can be included in the original financing package as an option subject to certain management performance targets. In all cases, the ability and willingness of co-investors to provide additional finance should be carefully judged when assembling a syndication team. This is because many of the practising venture capitalists interviewed described the difficulties they have had in attempting to get a syndicate partner to provide its pro-rata share of any second round financing. This may be particularly difficult where the syndicate partner is small, and therefore may be in danger of providing a disproportionate amount of its capital into a single investment. It can also prove to be a problem when a syndicate partner, due to its organisation or structure, has access to a finite or limited amount of capital. A venture capital fund raised via the Business Expansion Scheme (BES), for example, is a closed ended fund which may be fully invested with no access to additional capital.

Second round finance: conclusions

With respect to second round or follow-on finance the following conclusions can be drawn.

- As a shareholder rather than a creditor, it may be necessary to provide financing to an investee on more than one occasion prior to realisation.

- Notwithstanding the above, investors must be careful to avoid the 'if only...' syndrome. Second round and later (i.e. third and fourth round) financings should be supplied only if the additional capital commitment can be shown to have quantifiable benefits in the foreseeable future. Arguments of 'if only we had the working capital to last another three months...' must be judged with caution.

- In the case of syndicated investments, where an investor is the syndicate leader it must communicate the above point very clearly to its co-investors. Syndication partners should be selected bearing in mind their willingness and ability to provide additional capital when and where necessary.

Expansion capital

Many UK firms refer to themselves as 'development' rather than 'venture' capital providers. It is a means of showing where their activities lie in terms of the venture capital life cycle. Expansion and development are here used as synonymous terms.

Definition
Expansion capital refers to the finance provided to fund the expansion or growth of a company which is breaking even or trading at a small profit. Expansion or development capital will be used to finance increased production capacity, market or product development and/or to provide additional working capital.

Characteristics
Two broad categories of expansion capital can be identified:

- Investment in companies that have been substantially self-financed since foundation, and are seeking outside equity for the first time.

- The provision of second round finance to a company that has already received at least one round of early stage capital from other sources.

Companies seeking development finance for the first time will typically be more mature than those seeking second round finance, and sales of proven products normally tend to be at a higher level. These companies may well be able to continue without an injection of external capital, but the entrepreneur is perhaps attracted by the possibility to accelerate the company's growth or, in certain circumstances, to realise a part of his own equity. Firms of this nature may lend themselves easily to a trade sale. However, an initial placement on a public exchange may produce a better price.

Characteristics sought by UK venture capitalists in firms seeking expansion or development capital finance as stated by John Singer, Managing Director of Granville Europe SA, in a speech will be:

- A product range which has been developed and proven.

- An expanding level of production.

- A product range which has a competitive advantage in an identified market niche.

- A track record of sufficient length that the product will have become established and reasonable margins obtained.

- Profits in the range of £250,000 to £1,000,000.

Characteristics of venture capital investment at this stage of development are:

- Returns which will tend to be lower than for earlier stages of venture investment.

- Financing needs which will typically be larger than for earlier stages.

- Returns from investment which will typically be realised sooner.

Term to realisation
Expansion capital investors are normally looking for realisation within a two to five year time frame.

Expansion capital: volume of investment activity

The expansion capital market is characterised by a large number of players (including all of the bank-captive venture firms) as it is perceived to be an attractive market in terms of the risk versus reward trade off. Of the 147 firms surveyed by Peat Marwick in the study mentioned on p. 39, 140 (95%) stated that they were definitely involved in the provision of expansion or development capital, while another 4 responded that they would provide it under certain circumstances.

Expansion capital accounted for 47% of the financings provided in the

Year	Expansion Capital Investments	Investments as % of Total	Expansion Capital Invested £m	Value as % of Total	Expan. Cap. Average Investment (in £m)
1988	639	47.1	402.0	30.9	629,100
1987	631	52.2	274.9	29.4	435,700
1986	287	45.2	104.0	27.1	362,400
1985	259	47.7	104.0	38.5	401,000

Table 2.4 *Expansion capital as proportion of total UK venture finance – 1985 to 1988 (Figures from the BVCA)*

UK in 1988, representing 31% of the total by value. (Refer to Table 2.4.)

Expansion capital: features and risks

The nuance between *venture* and *development* capital is particularly observed by the large City-based bank captive firms which do not see themselves in the venture or in the – in their eyes – 'risk' capital business. The term development is a notable inclusion in the corporate titles of both Lloyd's and Barclay's unquoted equity investment arms. Nevertheless, expansion capital propositions are expected to clear a minimum 40% ROI hurdle rate.

Most of the UK venture capital firms active in the expansion capital market are relatively hands-off (in terms of day-to-day involvement with the investee). The majority, as previously noted, opt for Board level representation.

A distinguishing feature of the development as opposed to the venture investors is the tendency for the former to have financial skills (i.e. banking, accountancy) as opposed to line management or operational skills. This may explain the relatively hands-off nature of their portfolio management styles.

Another distinguishing feature of this stage of financing is the high proportion of investors who are seeking dividend or interest income from their investment, either by way of preference shares or through the topping up of their equity participation with subordinated debt.

The stock market crash of October 1987 may have improved expansion capital opportunities. The lower price : earnings multiples caused by the crash has dampened the IPO market and the ensuing wariness of the public equity markets generally will suppress the enthusiasm of the market for new issues. At the same time, the lower P : E multiples may provide the venture capitalist with better opportunities for buying into a company on preferential terms.

Expansion capital: conclusions

The following conclusions are made with respect to expansion capital investing:

- If the investor is seeking current income as well as capital gains, a portfolio of appropriately structured expansion capital investments would be attractive.

- While many expansion capital investments may be larger than many investors may wish to consider (note the average investment size of £629,000 in 1988), the ability to syndicate this type of investment is high, due to the large number of venture capitalists interested in financing expansion stage firms.

- This stage of investment will probably be more attractive to investors than other stages, in view of its relatively shorter maturity.

8

Management buy-outs, management buy-ins, and mezzanine financing

Management buy-outs

Few forms of venture capital investment have experienced either the volume of publicity or the dramatic growth of the management buy-out. The management buy-out is one of the preferred forms of venture investment by large venture capital funds in the UK.

Definition

A management buy-out (MBO) involves the acquisition of a company (or the shares in that company) from the existing owners by a team of existing management/employees. The vending shareholder may or may not have been actively involved in the running of the company, the acquiring group are presumed to be actively involved in the day-to-day running of the company and are making the acquisition with a view towards becoming active owner-managers.

The British Venture Capital Association defines the management buy-out as:

> Funds provided to enable current operating management and investors to acquire an existing product line or business. (Report on Investment Activities, 1987.)

Professional firms, such as lawyers and accountants, have been changing hands for years as senior partners are succeeded through the acquisition of their shares by former subordinates. While buyers with cash, credit and credibility had been acquiring businesses for decades, these were localised to unincorporated businesses, notably in low capital sectors such as the professions and service industries. What distinguishes the current MBO boom are the acquisitions, with control passing to management, of large scale manufacturing companies and other going concerns involving significant assets.

MBOs: characteristics

The management buy-out has much in common with, and a number of differences from, other forms of venture finance such as start-up or development capital. The common aspects of MBOs and other forms of venture capital finance are:

- MBOs are corporate finance, in the form of equity, in situations where the ability to obtain debt may be constrained due to the high level of gearing that would occur.

- MBO finance is above all else an investment into the management of the investee firm.

- MBOs require the surrender of a portion of management's equity, in return for finance from the venture capitalist. Although the venture capitalist may be supplying some debt component to the acquisition, it is through the equity that he hopes eventually to make his gains.

The differences, which can create additional or different risks, are noted in the section entitled 'MBOs: Features and Risks' which follows.

The MBO is a very late stage form of venture finance. As such, it typically involves less risk than some other stages. In assessing MBO opportunities, venture capital investors typically seek three characteristics of the investee firm:

- Proven management.

- A history of profitability.

- A history of market share.

MBOs: term to realisation

MBOs, unless followed by a period of asset stripping by the new owners, will typically take two or three years to fruition.

MBOs: volume of investment activity

Management buy-outs dwarf all other stages of UK venture capital activity in terms of value invested. (Refer to Table 2.5.) In 1988, the member firms of the British Venture Capital Association invested in 282 MBOs, more than any other stage of financing except expansion finance. Separate research, done on behalf of 3i, puts the recent volume of MBO activity even higher.

In 1988, for the second year running, MBO activity represented more than half the value of all venture capital investing by the members of the BVCA. This was due to the large average investment required to finance an MBO.

The buy-out phenomenon has shown remarkable growth in the UK over the past decade. The number of buy-outs, as reported by the Centre for Management Buy-out Research at Nottingham University, has increased at a rate of 40% per year since 1980. (Refer to Figure 2.2(a) and (b).)

Given the MBO's track record and the apparent benefits and advantages to all concerned, UK venture capitalists and financial institutions have shown themselves anxious to provide funds for buy-outs. Without doubt, the leader in MBO financing is 3i, which is widely seen to be the pioneer of MBO financing in the UK.

3i is perceived to be, and if deal volume is a proxy for expertise, it is the UK expert of MBO financings. It claims to have participated in more

Year	MBO Investments	MBOs as % of Total	MBO Capital Invested £m	MBO Value as % of Total	MBOs Average Investment
1988	282	20.8	733.0	56.4	£2,599,300
1987	199	16.5	480.1	51.5	£2,412,600
1986	131	20.6	173.6	45.2	£1,325,200
1985	91	16.8	100.8	37.3	£1,107,700

Table 2.5 *Management buy-outs as proportion of total UK venture finance – 1985 to 1988*
(Figures from the BVCA)

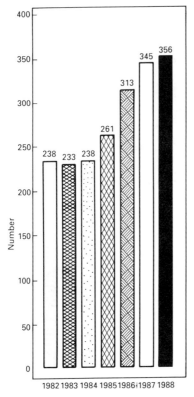

Figure 2.2a Number of management buy-outs in the UK 1982–1988. (Figures from the Centre for Management Buy-out Research)

than 600 such financings during the past decade, which means that it would have been involved in more than 40% of all deals.

MBOs: features

The rationale most often cited for the management buy-out is that it offers a company's management team the motivation and the satisfaction of running the business which gives them their living. MBOs are also said to offer certain advantages to:

- the seller (existing shareholders);
- the workforce;

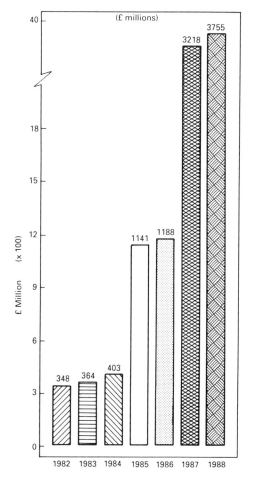

Figure 2.2b Value of Management buy-outs in the UK 1982–1988. (Figures from the Centre for Management Buy-out Research)

- customers and suppliers.

For the seller the management buy-out provides an opportunity to shed unwanted or no longer strategically important assets to an informed, experienced and generally friendly acquirer. The MBO is one transaction where the buyer probably understands the item for sale and its value better than the seller. This, it is claimed, facilitates a quick and relatively quiet sale without some of the costs, uncertainties and morale problems which might be associated with hostile takeover bids and other forms of divestment. An example of one such MBO is the £160 million acquisition of the Compass Group from Grand Metropolitan in May 1987.

To the workforce, a management buy-out – even if the new share-holders are restricted to a small number of more senior managers – will probably be perceived as a better alternative than new ownership. Existing senior management should have a better understanding of the workforce than new, outside ownership. (This is not to claim that they will be any less disposed toward employment cuts.)

To customers and suppliers, buy-out by a company's existing manage-ment means no loss in continuity of contact, and no need to seek new sources of supply.

To an institutional investor, funding MBOs presents the opportunity to realise superior returns through a combination of large spreads (typically 300 to 400 basis points) on the highly levered debt as well as capital gains from equity participation.

Management buy-outs generally occur for one of four reasons:

- *Divergence from the group's interests.* The company to be acquired belongs to a larger group, with diversified interests. While the subsidiary or division may still enjoy profitability, it may no longer fit in with the larger organisation's longer term strategic goals or mainstream activities. An example of this is the £28.5 million acquisition of Clare Equipment in 1987 from Guinness, a financing arranged by Security Pacific Hoare Govett.

- *Retirement of a shareholder-partner.* A private company may belong wholly or mainly to an active shareholder-partner who is contemplat-ing retirement. Rather than wind up the business, the existing owner may wish to pass on his equity to key employees, perpetuating the company. A total of 192 MBOs were recorded by the periodical *Acquisitions Monthly* during the first ten months of 1987. Of these, some 33 or 17% were MBOs initiated by an owner-manager who wished to retire.

- *Problems within the parent organisation.* An enterprise may be a division or subsidiary of an ailing conglomerate. Problems within the parent may lead to a siphoning-off of cash necessary to maintain steady growth, it may lead to inconsistent or detrimental decision making at the very top, it may lead to timidity in seizing growth opportunities by head office management immersed in rationalization. Once acquired from the existing owners, the independently run firm may yield superior returns. An example of this is the acquisition of Parker Pen, from its former owners, Manpower.

- *As a defence strategy*. Most recently, management buy-outs have been used by management as a defensive strategy against hostile takeovers.

While there are a large number of similarities, the management buy-out can differ from most types of venture opportunity in a variety of ways. The company to be acquired need not be new or small, as in most venture capital opportunities. Indeed, it can be a large, well-established company with a long track record and current earnings and the firm to be acquired may also enjoy a public listing. Largely as a consequence of the latter the buy-out is distinguished from other forms of venture capital investment in that it involves substantially larger sums of money. In 1986, of the 261 buy-outs reported, 24 transactions were valued at more than £10 million. These, however, accounted for 72% of the buy-outs by value.

Unlike most venture capital investment, a management buy-out pre-supposes the existence of a full management team in place and, finally, an MBO financing may be viewed as hostile by existing share-holders.

MBOs: risks

Despite their rather impressive track record and the evident attractions of appropriately targeted and structured MBOs, they are not without their risks and pitfalls. Indeed, many venture capitalists express growing reluctance to become involved in more MBO financings.

The risk highlighted by many venture capitalists is a *me too* mentality. Management buy-outs have undoubtedly become fashionable amongst providers of corporate financial services. This may have led to an excess of finance being made available for MBOs. Approximately £5 billion worth of funds are now available to finance buy-outs in the UK twice the amount actually invested in 1988.

The danger of funds being so readily available is that MBOs may be undertaken by inadequate management teams. One of the biggest problems facing these teams is the sudden realisation that corporate-wide services and facilities once taken for granted (including access to large scale financial resources) are no longer available.

Another reason for MBOs in less than ideal situations is that they often take place on the instigation of corporate finance teams of merchant banks rather than the company management. It has been said that bankers are now chasing buy-outs the way they once chased sovereign borrowers in the third world, and to the same probable effect. We see deals which are completely dependent on assets being sold off after one or two years. If there is a slump in the market or a rise in interest rates they are dead.

The popularity of the buy-out among financial institutions has meant an increase in the price of these deals (sellers recognising the liquidity of the buy-out market) and an increase in the size of the equity and debt package that management can demand from the providers of outside capital. The typical UK buy-out is financed with a gearing of 4 : 1. Even this is conservative in relation to US buy-out activity where the investor's debt is often levered eight or nine times. Beatrice Corporation, the largest MBO ever accomplished, was financed by US$600 million in equity and US$5.4 billion in debt.

The MBO market appears to have become a buyers' market (management as buyer and venture capitalist as seller of financial services) which seems to have reduced the return on equity flowing to venture capitalists and institutional backers of buy-out funds.

The five year bull market which collapsed in October 1987 pushed up the market value of subsidiary companies and the asking price of enterprises trading in businesses currently enjoying high multiples. In Canada, many venture capitalists began to avoid MBOs in late 1986. They cited buy-outs which had been done at three and four times book value, and shares for IPOs which had been trading at more than twenty times earnings.

The combination of high asking price, the availability of ample funds for MBOs and the desire of corporate finance groups to become involved in MBO financing leads to the danger that willing entrepreneur-managers will pay too much for the acquired assets. A Director of 3i, has been quoted in the *Financial Times* to say that his fund will begin to avoid backing any management buy-outs. The reasons cited were those mentioned above:

• unreasonably high multiples;

- an excess of easily obtainable finance;
- a track record that may be too good to sustain.

Certainly, the buy-out phenomenon is a cyclical one, with economic conditions during the mid-80s being unusually accommodating to the would be buy-out. These benign conditions include the combination of falling interest rates, high consumption, and a rising equity market. This enabled the buyer to borrow relatively large amounts of capital in the expectation that sales would continue to increase interest payments would fall, and the multiple of price to ever increasing earnings would grow. As the stock market collapse of October 1987 proved, this was an unrealistic expectation. Since the spring of 1988 interest rates have followed a dramatic uphill course. The Base Rate, at 7.5% during summer 1988, doubled to 15% by October 1989 thus putting to test the wisdom of many highly geared MBOs.

Management buy-ins

A management buy-in involves bringing in a management team of outsiders, strangers to the company, as opposed to a buy-out where they were part of the existing team.

Definition
The British Venture Capital Association defines the management buy-in as:

> Funds provided to enable a manager or group of managers from outside the company to buy-in to the company with the support of venture capital investors. (*Report on Investment Activity*, 1986)

While the buy-in shares common factors with the better known buy-out there are distinct differences. It shares the combination of an investor or group of investors, which provide the bulk of finance, and a management team which takes an equity stake and frequently options to reward performance.

Characteristics
Both buy-outs and buy-ins characteristically inherit a heavy load of debt which must be paid off as rapidly as possible with cash flow from operations or from asset disposal.

Four elements are essential to the successful management buy-in:

- *A management team with a successful track record*, preferably in the same industry as the company they are taking over. Experience of managing an independent company, rather than of just running a subsidiary of a larger group, is also an advantage. Ideally, the managers will have previously carried a buy-out of the company for which they worked.

- *An existing management which is willing to stay in place* and work with incoming management as a team, during the transition period of a year or two.

- *An investor able to judge a good management team and willing* to take on the higher risk associated with buy-ins compared with buy-outs. The investor must also be ready to be closely involved with the management team.

- *A target company which is underperforming* because of weak management. It may be a subsidiary or an independent company, either private or public, with a management or shareholders who want to sell out.

Management buy-ins: volume of investment activity

Hand-in-hand with the management buy-out, the management buy-in has seen a rise in its recognition among venture capital providers in the UK. However, a total of just 94 management buy-ins took place in Britain in 1987, which shows that buy-ins lag far behind buy-outs in popularity.

Number of Buy-ins	Buy-ins as % of Total	Value of Buy-ins (£m)	Buy-ins as % of Total	Avg. Value
18	1.5	£32.9	3.5	£1,828,000

Table 2.6 *Management buy-ins as proportion of total UK venture finance –
1987*
(Figures from BVCA)

British Venture Capital Association data indicate similar orders of magnitude. In 1987, the first year for which separate data on MBIs were obtained, MBIs represented just 1.5% of total BVCA financings. (Refer to Table 2.6.)

Management buy-ins: features and risks

The risks involved in attempting a management buy-in are numerous. There is likely to be a higher casualty rate than with management buy-outs as teams of new managers, who may not have worked together before, go into industries with which they are not likely to be intimately familiar. This places an extra premium on management skills and on management's ability to respond to the problems of the company they are joining. Another danger to the success of management buy-ins is a possible clash of cultures between managers being parachuted in, and an ingrained work force, unused to the slick management techniques of the high-flyers, the company doctors, and the turn-around specialists.

Finally, the new managers are likely to hit upon problems within the acquired company which have gone undetected, no matter how thorough the pre-acquisition analysis.

To the venture financier, the management buy-in poses additional work requirements in that due diligence must be performed twice, both on the investee company and on the management separately, with the additional burden of further analysing the synergy (or otherwise) to be obtained from the marriage of the two.

In discussions within the venture finance community, the prevailing opinion was that the management buy-in phenomenon is substantially exaggerated by the financial press. Other than 3i, few of the venture capital firms interviewed claimed significant expertise in buy-in financing, or more than a short track record.

Most recently, 3i is establishing a register of would-be buy-in managers, and is prepared to train potential buy-in candidates. It has set up a dedicated team of 12 responsible for developing buy-in business in the UK and hopes to establish a 'stable' of some 200 managers who it sees as likely candidates for buying into likely situations that its buy-in team will identify.

The buy-in appears to be a case of supply driving demand, at least in so far as the number of would-be providers of MBI finance are concerned. Many UK venture capitalists have raised doubts as to the cultural ability of UK managers to buy-in to 'risk' situations, other venture capitalists maintain there simply does not exist sufficient depth of management talent.

Mezzanine finance

The last stage of equity related funding is so-called mezzanine finance.

Definition
The term mezzanine is used for two reasons:

- it is a half-way stage between equity and loan capital in terms of risk and return;

- it is often the last financing supplied to a private company in the final run up to a trade sale or a public flotation.

Mezzanine financing is supplied as a layer which ranks behind secured lending but before ordinary share capital. Thus, mezzanine funding may be supplied either as debt (high coupon bonds) or as high ranking equity (preference shares). To compensate for the greater risk attached to unsecured lending, or the lack of voting power in preference shares, recipients of mezzanine financing must offer a higher rate of return than to secured lenders. Typically, mezzanine funds expect to earn 300 to 400 basis points more than secured loans or senior debt.

Characteristics
Suppliers of mezzanine finance point to the following characteristics of mezzanine capital which distinguish it from investments in ordinary share capital, and which make it more attractive as a venture capital investment:

- when structuring an MBO, the provision of mezzanine finance allows management a greater share of business than would otherwise be afforded;

- being lower risk than ordinary share capital, it requires a lower rate of return;

- if provided by way of debt, it has tax advantages;

- it can be secured.

Term to realisation

Mezzanine financing is intended as a form of bridge finance. Typically, therefore, it is expected to have a maturity of less than two years.

Mezzanine finance: features and risks

Discussion of mezzanine financing is included here not only because it can assume the form of preference capital but also because this type of funding may carry an equity bonus, in the form of options or warrants.

The combination of a high running yield and a package of options and warrants is expected to take the overall yield on mezzanine finance to between 20% and 26% per year. Particularly attractive to suppliers of development capital is the fact that the debt component of mezzanine finance will provide a positive carry from day one, pacifying share holders in the interim before the equity options can be exercised to give truly superior returns.

Mezzanine financing can be used to afford a management buy-out team with little capital to acquire a large equity stake in their company while providing the investor with a return commensurate with the risks.

The fact that mezzanine financing involves both debt and equity makes it of interest to the bank-captive venturer. The large (300 to 400 basis points) spreads make this type of financing of particular interest to the financial institution which is intent on maintaining or raising its net income margin from lending activities. While the subordinated nature of the debt is perhaps contrary to a bank's normal lending policies, the equity participation affords significant profit potential to offset the risk.

9

Summary

It is important to recognise that the term venture capital investment includes a variety of approaches to unlisted equity finance. In Part two, seven different stages of venture capital investment were identified. These were differentiated in terms of the stage of the investee company's development and, generally, in terms of the length of time to realisation on the investment.

The seven stages of venture investment identified were:

- seed capital
- start-up capital
- early stage finance
- second round finance
- expansion capital
- management buy-outs and buy-ins
- mezzanine finance

In the discussion of each, a definition was offered, as were their characteristics, the approximate term to realisation, the features and risks and, where available, some recent statistics on the volume of investment activity in each stage of the venture capital life cycle.

The purpose of this section of the text is to identify the various segments in the demand for venture finance.

Seed capital. Few UK venture capital firms seem inclined to provide seed capital. Certainly, the value of this type of venture capital finance is small when compared to the total value of investment from all stages. Reasons cited for the absence of significant seed capital investment are that such propositions tend to be too small, too long to fruition, and often too technology oriented for the investment portfolios of most venture capital firms.

Start-up capital. As with seed capital, few venture capital investors appear to be very interested in providing start-up capital. The amounts involved in each investment tend to be small and the term to realisation long.

Early stage finance. This is the earliest stage in a company's development when the majority of fundamentals are in place: management team assembled, product developed, market identified. Opportunities for highly profitable investment continue since start-up companies continue to lack either the cash flow or the earnings record often required as a condition for attracting debt finance. More venture capital providers appear to be interested in providing early stage finance than either seed or start-up capital, so syndication and take-out opportunities exist.

Second round finance. It is typically after the early stage of a company's development that management will require an additional injection of capital. The provision of second round or 'follow-on' finance is an accepted part of the venture capital investment process. Moreover, the entrepreneur expects it. Investors must recognise that the first injection of capital into a growth firm will not necessarily be the last. They must be prepared to invest accordingly.

Expansion capital. Expansion, or development capital is typically used to accelerate the growth of a small firm already in the growth stage of its development. With a realisation horizon of three to five years, expansion capital is generally more acceptable to bank-captive venture capital providers than earlier forms of venture finance. This is a form of venture capital which is well populated by suppliers and offers high rewards for reasonable risks.

Management buy-outs. The management buy-out is the most popular form of venture capital finance, and now accounts for more than half the value of all venture capital investment in the UK. The buy-out appears ideally suited to bank-captive venture capital providers since it combines equity investment normally geared by significant amounts of debt. Bank-captive venture capital firms are the leading providers of MBO finance, and profess to realise superior returns (30% per annum) in return for only moderate risks. Recently however, concern has been expressed of the excess supply of MBO capital in relation to demand. Many venture capital firms have now begun to shun what they see as an over-priced, over-publicised financial mechanism.

Management buy-ins. The management buy-in in the UK is still in its infancy. Few MBI deals have been done on any scale and many venture capitalists view the growth of management buy-in activity as illusory. The risks of the management buy-in are compounded by the need to evaluate management, business, and the marriage of the two.

Mezzanine finance. This form of venture finance is more akin to traditional bank lending than the other forms that have been mentioned. Offering lower yields and shorter terms than most forms of venture capital equity investment, mezzanine finance combines equity with debt or subordinated debt packages which offer significant spreads. This later stage form of unlisted equity finance appears to be less popular among venture capital providers than the MBO.

As a final conclusion, it is noted that a positive relationship exists between the stage of company development and both the total and average value of the venture investment. This is due to the increased financing needs of the larger investee and the higher minimum investment floor of the larger players who occupy this market.

Part three

Entrepreneur expectations and investor requirements

10

Analysing venture capital proposals

The venture capital process begins when an entrepreneur, either wishing to start up a new company or seeking to expand or acquire an existing one, decides to raise external capital.

For companies seeking seed, start-up or early stage finance, traditional forms of company finance – such as bank loans or lines of credit – may be difficult to obtain. The very youngest or smallest of companies may lack the requisites of bank credit, i.e. sufficient working capital or cash flow to support short term finance, or the assets to secure long term finance. Alternatively, finance seekers may have attracted but exhausted, a supply of debt finance. This is most likely the case with firms seeking second round or development capital.

Entrepreneurs wishing to finance buy-outs or buy-ins probably seek venture capital funding for non-financial reasons: advice and support, industry contacts and perhaps because they perceive venture capitalists as more entrepreneurial, more risk oriented, more attracted by the potential returns than providers of debt finance.

Whatever their motivation for raising equity, the most likely first contact between the entrepreneur and the venture capital investor will be the business plan.

This Chapter briefly considers the business plan, its purpose, and the analytical processes that a venture capital company will use in evaluating the investment propositions which cross its threshold.

The business plan

A business plan is a document which is fundamental to the process of introducing an entrepreneur and his business to the venture capitalist. Simply stated, a business plan is a formal, written proposal for the raising of external capital. It is the first, and therefore the most important contact between a would-be investor and a manager seeking to raise funds for his firm. The purpose of a written business plan is two-fold. On the one hand it can help the entrepreneur to crystallise his ideas. On the other hand, the venture capitalist uses the business plan to compare that firm's investment proposal with a selection of competing investment opportunities. The business plan will make an inventory of the company's strengths and weaknesses, identify the keys to success or failure, and itemise the resources (financial or otherwise) that it will need to go forward.

We noted in Chapter 3 that very few business proposals actually reach the stage where they are successful in attracting outside equity. We saw that, typically, most venture capitalists finance less than 5% of the propositions they receive. This is because the decision to proceed, and ultimately to invest, hinges on four criteria, each of which must be satisfied before the venture capitalist will commit his funds. The four criteria are:

- fundamental analysis as to the soundness of the business;

- financial analysis of the prospect for the value of the business to grow;

- portfolio analysis to determine whether the investment will fit into the venture capitalist's 'basket' of investments;

- divestment analysis to determine the means, timing and probable value of the investment upon 'exit'.

Let us consider each of them in turn:

Fundamental analysis

Fundamental analysis refers to an examination of the basic or fundamental aspects of the business without which the investor cannot even begin to make an informed investment decision. The fundamental analysis will, at a minimum, consider the following:

- A brief history of the company including date of incorporation and summary of progress to date.

- The quality, experience, strategy and motivations of management, directors and existing shareholders.

- A complete description of the company's products or services. This will consider the distinctive advantages or unique selling points which will lead to the company's success.

- The markets which the company serves, including size and nature of the industry; the size, location and characteristics of the customer base; potential competition; and distinctive or unique selling points.

- Manufacturing and operational aspects of the business, including a description of the technology employed, access to sources of supply, manufacturing capacity, and the premises owned or occupied.

- An objective analysis of the fundamental risks and management's plans to cope with these.

Financial analysis

The purpose of the financial projections in a business plan is to set out the financial implications of a company's strategy and to measure its performance. The projections should correspond to and complement the narrative parts of the business plan.

In analysing the company's financial projections, the venture capitalist will be looking to determine:

- the earnings growth potential of the company;

- the sensitivity of these earnings to fluctuations in sales and margins, (and therefore the risk associated with the return);

- the likely time-lag between investments (e.g. capital equipment, marketing or R&D) and return;

- the likely impact on cash flow, and the possibility of having to make second and third round financings into investees which do not live up to their projections;

- the expected value of the company at the notional time of divestment;

- an objective analysis of the financial risks and management's plans to cope with these.

Most venture capitalists evaluate proposals on the basis of their potential financial return on investment. This return, as we noted in Chapter 3, will be subject to discount rates (to account for the risk) and expected value calculations. Only after they have satisfied themselves that the business proposition bears an acceptable level of probability for an attractive rate of return will the business be deemed as an attractive prospective investment. The method of measurement most commonly used is internal rate of return (IRR).

The 40% IRR is comprised of two elements:-

a) Forfeited opportunity of not investing in
   other forms of investment (e.g. quoted
   securities)   10%

b) Allowance for risk (to include sensitivity
   analysis)   <u>30%</u> minimum

   REQUIRED RATE OF RETURN
   FROM AN INVESTMENT   40% +

Another essential factor in the decision process is the investee company's ability to interest other investors. While a heavy demand by venture capitalists is not necessarily indicative of the quality of a company, the reverse is likely to be true.

Portfolio analysis

Having cleared the hurdles of fundamental and financial analysis, the business plan must be perceived to 'fit'. The initial investment decision will also depend upon the venture capitalist's portfolio balance at the time the investment proposal is being considered. That is, the proposed investment must be an acceptable addition to the venture capitalist's portfolio in terms of its size, its stage of development, its geographic location and its industry sector. In Part Two, we considered the various stages of venture capital funding. It was noted that many venture capital firms avoid seed, start-up and early stage propositions for fundamental reasons, while a growing number of venture capitalists are becoming wary of the MBO market for reasons of finance (too much money chasing too few deals). In ensuing chapters we will examine recent trends in UK venture capital investment by size of investment, by country, by region and by sector, and consider some of the reasons why certain industries or locations receive more finance than others. For the present, let us consider some of the issues involved in portfolio selection and in the strategy of portfolio diversification.

Investment size

The first factor which the venture capital firm will typically include in its assessment will be a limit to the total amount of cash committed to any one company, regardless of the perceived risks and returns. Typically, most venture capital firms set this limit at 10% of the total pool of investable funds.

The amount invested per company can vary between a relatively small sum of money and several million pounds depending on the size of the fund and on the fund's strategy. The amount of money per investment has a significant impact on the size of the portfolio.

If the venture capitalist builds up a very large portfolio, hands-on management will be difficult. If it focuses the portfolio on a limited number of companies it can take care of the investee companies, but must take into account that a small portfolio is very sensitive to failures. In most cases it is not easy to find an adequate trade-off between a reasonable spread risk of and effective investment management.

Stage of development

The second aspect of portfolio diversification is to mix the stages of development. A venture capital portfolio will typically consist of some companies which are in the start-up phase, some companies in a development stage and other companies in a more mature phase of the life-cycle such as MBO investments. The rationale for such a diversified portfolio is the assumption that the risk of a failure is correlated to the age of the company.

First of all, this assumption is not necessarily always true and secondly, all these different stages need completely different skills and experience on the side of the venture capitalists. In start-up situations it is very important to understand the business. The venture capital manager shares the difficulties of the business with the entrepreneur, he visits the company regularly and he provides active support. The needs of a company in a later stage are completely different. Here the financial aspects are more important.

Geographic location
While significantly the largest in Europe, the domestic UK market may be regarded as small by the largest venture capital firms. In order to reach an acceptable level of portfolio diversity and volume, many funds will look to invest abroad. The basic principle of a successful international investment policy is to join a syndicate with a local fund, which will have a superior understanding the market, the social, investment, and tax environment. Because of the additional risks in investing off shore, the vast majority of UK based venture capital is invested domestically. For reasons of language and culture, the US ranks next.

One strategy for investing off shore is for the venture capital firm to focus on a limited number of industries, which will need less time to assess, and to gain a basic understanding of the market.

Industry sectors
The fourth factor in portfolio diversification is the mix of industry sectors. Here again, venture capital investors will attempt to diversify the portfolio in order to offset investments in problem or slow growth sectors with investments in sectors where more positive developments are occurring.

Divestment analysis

It is vital that the venture capitalist keeps his mind on the exit at all times. Prior to entering into any investment, the venture capitalist should have a clear idea as to the method, the timing and the valuation of the company upon divestment. These factors will need to be explicitly addressed at the time of making the investment decision.

There are four principal means by which the venture capitalist realises his investment. Let us now consider each of these:

- Trade sale

- Take out

- Earn out

- Flotation

Trade sale
The trade sale is simply the selling of the investment to a company in the

trade, i.e. a competitor wishing to buy the investee's market share or production capacity, a supplier looking to integrate forward, or a customer looking to integrate backward or tie up sources of supply.

A trade sale will typically come in the form of an unexpected and unsolicited bid. Selling out to a competitor should be a relatively smooth process since, in theory, the competitor will have some insight into the product and the market in which the enterprise is engaged. In a trade sale, it is likely that the bidder will want to buy some or all of the entrepreneur's shares, in addition to those of the venture capitalist.

Take out

The take out is the selling of the investment to another professional investor, another venture capitalist or perhaps by way of a private placement with a major institutional investor such as an insurance company or pension fund manager, or to a management holding company. In a take out, typically, only the venture capital company will sell its shares, the entrepreneur retaining his. Reasons for selling a profitable investment to another investor may include the need to increase or maintain the fund's liquidity or perhaps because the investee has passed from one stage of growth to another (from early stage to a later stage) where the venture capitalist no longer feels it can provide value or maintain the earnings growth realised early on.

Earn out

Another means of realising a venture capital investment is the earn-out, through which the entrepreneur buys back the venture capitalist's shares with the proceeds of his own earnings. Typically an earn out will be accomplished by the owner-manager buying a predetermined proportion of the venture capitalist's shares at a price negotiated in advance. Essentially, the entrepreneur will be given an option at the time of his investment. The option price of the shares will be set at a level which will satisfy the venture capital firm's hurdle rate.

Flotation

The final possible exit route is via a stock market flotation. The UK has established second and third markets with less restrictive conditions for flotations of medium sized companies than the full 'listed' exchange. So, not only large companies have the opportunity to raise public equity. For venture capitalists the second and third tier stock markets are a major way to realise their investment. (Refer to Chapter 24).

Of course not all companies are suitable for the flotation. The ideal company should be a multi-product company, it should be very secure in its products either by patents or by market share. Ideally, the company should have a good customer base and consistent profit growth rate. With an even profit growth it is much easier to achieve a good share price in an initial public offering (IPO).

In order to float the company must have a good, and complete, management team. At an early venture capital stage it might be possible to get along with gaps in the management, especially when the venture capital investor is active and can influence the entrepreneur-manager from a position of influence such as a seat on the Board. When the company goes public, however, all directors and managers must be in place.

The methods of flotation can vary. Generally, the following three are distinguished:

- *Placings*, where a company's shares are placed with pre-arranged buyers.

- *Offers for Sale*, where a company invites the public to subscribe for its shares at a fixed price which is underwritten.

- *Tender*, where the public is invited to name a number of shares and a price it will pay, with a minimum price underwritten.

What venture capitalists expect from entrepreneurs

Understanding the venture capitalist's decision-making criteria will provide a basis for early action by entrepreneurs to improve their success in attracting finance. We will now review some of the existing research which has sought to determine the attributes of investee companies seen as most important by venture capitalists.

Table 3.1 compares the rank ordering of deal selection criteria in two empirical studies carried out in the United States in the 1970s. Wells (1974) focused on criteria which evaluate managerial abilities and other qualitative characteristics of the enterprise. Poindexter (1976), on the other hand, favoured criteria which reflected financial characteristics.

Wells (1974)	Poindexter (1976)
1. Management Commitment	1. Quality of Management
2. Product	2. Expected Rate of Return
3. Market	3. Expected Risk
4. Management Marketing Skill	4. Percent of Equity Owned
5. Management Engineering Skill	5. Management Financial Commitment
6. Marketing Plan	6. Financial Controls & Provisions
7. Management Financial Skill	7. Venture Stage
8. Management Manufacturing Skill	8. Financial Restrictive Covenants
9. Recommendations/References	9. Interest/Dividend Rate
10. Participators in Deal	10. Asset Security as Collateral
11. Industry/Technology	11. Present Capitalisation
12. Cash-out Method	12. Investor Control
	13. Tax Shelter Considerations

Table 3.1 *Rank order to importance of deal selection criteria*
(Source: Tyebjee and Bruno)

Note that *Management Commitment* and *Quality of Management* were the first ranking criteria in both studies.

Hoban (1976) examined the rate of return actually achieved on venture capital invested in 50 firms and the attributes of each of the investee companies. Three characteristics were significantly related to the rate of return achieved:

Negative Factors

Proportion of equity not owned by the entrepreneur.

Positive Factors

Stage of product development.
Extensiveness of market research.

Here again, management commitment (as reflected by the size of entrepreneur's stake) is a key determinant of success.

Tyebjee and Bruno (1981) researched two separate aspects of the venture capital decision making process. First, they examined venture capitalists' perceptions of the business plans crossing their desks. Their findings were as follows:

1. Solicited deals were more likely to be funded than unsolicited deals.

2. Entrepreneurs who work full-time with the proposed venture and who have general management, as opposed to specific functional area skills, are more likely to attract finance.

3. Entrepreneurs who have not made a full-time commitment to a venture are less likely to attract finance.

4. The size of the deal affects the decision.

5. Medium-sized deals, in the range of $0.5 to $1.5 million, were viewed more favourably than those which involved more or less finance.

6. Product newness and development stage had no impact on the decision, nor did the stage of the venture.

Second, Tyebjee & Bruno's research established six factors used by venture capitalists in evaluating deals:

1. Management Quality

2. Profitability

3. Cash-out Factors

4. Venture Viability

5. Market Factors

6. Uncontrollable Risk Protection

A recent article from the *Journal of Business Venturing* listed ten factors relating to the success of a new venture. These were:

The percentage of founders who have held positions similar to those they assume in the new company.

The percentage of founders who have previously worked in high growth organisations.

The degree of completeness of the founders' management team at the time of funding.

The degree of prior joint experience among the founders.

The projected market share targeted by the new company; successful companies target a significantly higher market share than unsuccessful ones. In particular, successful companies look to gain high market share by carving out market niches.

The 'price performance' of the product relative to the competition.

The level of detail in planning the development of the technology.

The more successful companies operate in a market where there is a relatively small number of potential customers with each customer having a large buying capacity.

Successful companies target market segments relatively uninhabited by strong competitors or avoid head on competition with firms already established in that market.

Finally, the percentage of equity held by the venture capitalist(s) does not affect the success of the investee company.

While each of these surveys was conducted in the United States, the underlying features of all of these surveys are probably true for venture capital investment on both sides of the Atlantic.

What entrepreneurs expect from venture capitalists

As we saw in the previous chapter, a wealth of material exists on the criteria used by venture capitalists in making their investment decisions. On the other hand, less has been written on the expectations held by entrepreneurs and the criteria they use when first approaching and then having to choose between two or more sources of venture capital finance.

Conventional wisdom maintains that entrepreneurs are expecting value added from venture capitalists, primarily in three ways: through the provision of advice, through the provision of contacts, and through introduction to additional amounts of capital.

Survey of entrepreneurial firms

To obtain a better understanding of the demands of entrepreneurs and the needs of those firms, the author surveyed 93 venture capital backed companies located throughout the UK. The survey was intended to determine their attitudes, their expectations, and the attributes they consider to be important when seeking to find an equity investor-partner.

The purpose of this chapter is to provide the reader with a knowledge and understanding of the advice and assistance that entrepreneurial firms expect their venture capital firm to provide.

Venture capital is a package of services

An essential element of the definition of venture capital is that venture capital requires hands-on management. In Chapter 2, this aspect of the venture capital product was examined primarily from the viewpoint of the supplier, the venture capitalists themselves. Among the reasons for providing active, hands-on portfolio management, the following factors were identified:

- *Venture capital investments tend to be highly illiquid.* Unlike many other forms of finance, equity investments in unincorporated ventures generally cannot be sold on a secondary market, thus cutting losses. The equity investor is therefore faced both with a long term investment and an investment from which there exists no ready means of exit.

- *Short term downturns in small companies with large capital requirements can have terminal results.* Even in the event of turnaround or recovery, it is unlikely that positive returns will be realised before a number of years. Therefore, when a venture capital financing is made, the investor may often find a very real need to take an active, long term role in managing its investment.

- *Many small businesses are founded by entrepreneurs and technologists.* These owner-managers often lack either the skills or the inclination to manage a growth company. Frequently, the deficiency lies in the area of financial management and control. The venture capital manager must be prepared to complement the existing management team, or identify likely candidates who can.

- *The investee company expects and wants it.* In return for surrendering a portion of his equity, the entrepreneur will be seeking benefits beyond those normally supplied by a more passive investor. The provision of expertise and advice will often be one of the key reasons that the entrepreneur will seek equity, as opposed to debt capital.

This last reason forms the core of this chapter and we will now explore it further.

The provision of advice

When asked whether they expected venture capitalists to provide up-front advice, firms were evenly split in their expectations. Fifty-three percent of respondents indicated that they felt a venture capital firm should provide advice prior to an investment being made. Forty-seven percent had no such expectation. This seems to confirm the impression that entrepreneurs are innovative but may lack some management ability.

Stage of Development	% of Mentions
Start-Up	66.6
Early Stage	63.6
Growth	22.2

Table 3.2 *Entrepreneur's expectations concerning the provision of up-front advice stage of corporate development*

Slightly more than half of the entrepreneurs questioned appeared conscious of the need for upfront input from the venture capitalist.

The issue of upfront advice was further examined in relation to the stage of development at which investee companies originally sought venture capital finance. As much as 66.6% of start-ups, and 63.6% of early stage companies, expected up-front advice. Only 22.2% of companies receiving venture capital in their growth stage also expected up-front advice.

The obvious conclusion is that companies at later stages of development are less likely to be seeking up-front advice. For those companies seeking venture capital at their growth stage, the need for up-front advice has been alleviated. These firms have much of their organisational structure and operational routine in place already. While external advice may be sought on such issues as expanding into new products and new markets, more established firms see themselves as having less need for advice than younger firms.

Entrepreneurs expect venture capital firms to assist in validating the risk/reward ratio, to help in perfecting the business plan and, to a slightly lesser extent, to assist in analysing the idea. Among unprompted responses, some firms indicated that they felt that a venture capital firm should provide up-front financial advice.

The reader must be wary in distinguishing between those firms which do not require much in the way of outside advice and those which spurn such advice at their own (and the investor's) peril. Approximately one half of the entrepreneur-managers surveyed indicated that they did not expect the provider of venture capital to offer up-front advice. No distinction is made between those who feel that it is not 'part of the package', those who genuinely are in no need of up-front support, and those who are unreceptive to advice whether needed or not.

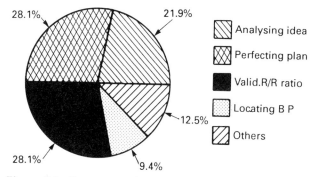

Figure 3.1 Entrepreneurs' expectations concerning the nature of up-front advice

Most venture capitalists believe in the need for 'hands-on' portfolio management. Usually this is accomplished by taking a position on the Board of Directors of the investee firm.

In a survey conducted by the author firms were asked to indicate the role they expected the venture capital executive to play in the running of the company. Three options were offered:

- *Active Advisor* – implying an active Board member who participates much as a management consultant with executive capacity.

- *Non-Executive idea-sounding Director* – implying a passive sounding board for the entrepreneur-manager.

- *No Participation* – implying a non-interfering relationship with investments requiring only periodic accounts and reports.

Confirming the suppliers' view, the overwhelming majority of the firms surveyed expected their venture capital executive to take a role in the management of the company. The preferred form of participation was at the Board level, where the venture capitalist can play the role of sounding board. A more active role was expected from nearly a quarter of firms, while only three out of 32 respondents expected the venture capital firm to take no participation at all.

Again, growth firms were less prepared to accept a venture capitalist in an active capacity than firms at an earlier stage of development. One third of those firms which described themselves as start-ups when first seeking finance indicated a willingness for active advice. By contrast, only 10% of firms in the growth stage of their development sought or expected active advice.

Nature of Role	Start-Up %	Early Growth %	Growth %
Active Advisor	33	36	10
Non-Exec. Idea-Sounding	67	55	90
No Participation	00	09	00
Total	100	100	100

Table 3.3 *Entrepreneurs' expectations as to role of venture capital executive stage of corporate development*

The vast majority of entrepreneurial firms fully expect that their venture capital investor will take part in the overall management of the company. It is clear, however, that venture capitalists are expected to take a Board level, as opposed to a day-to-day management position.

Not unexpectedly, the more mature the investee company the less hands-on will be the role expected of the venture capitalist. This probably reflects both a growing confidence on the part of the management of the growing firm, but also a decreasing need for external management support as the investee develops its own internal resources.

Nature of advice

When asked about the nature of the advice that they expect, entrepreneurs show a desire for strategic and financial advice. Perhaps surprisingly, only a small number mentioned marketing advice. The unprompted responses sought assistance in identifying market opportunities, identifying further sources of capital, and assisting in the creation of strategic alliances.

These results confirm those of recent work done by Leyshon and Turner in interviewing a sample of small businesses in Scotland as to their perceived needs for advice. In that study, while 'strategic' advice was not offered as an option, financial advice was overwhelmingly identified by small business managers as their main area of weakness. As with the present study, 'marketing' and 'technical' advice were deemed to be significantly less important.

Clearly, strategic and financial advice are the areas where entrepreneurs perceive they are most in need of assistance. The relatively low number of mentions of 'marketing' may suggest either a high degree of

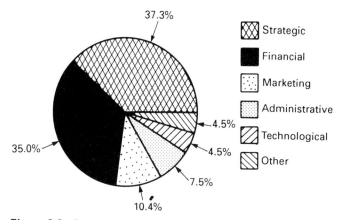

Figure 3.2 Entrepreneurs' expectations concerning the nature of post-investment advice

confidence on the part of entrepreneurs as to their marketing skills and resources. Alternatively, the failure to identify marketing as an area where advice may be required could suggest a lack of awareness on the part of many entrepreneurs as to the importance of this key business function. It will therefore be the venture capitalist's job to educate the entrepreneur so as to recognise areas where expertise may be required.

The provision of contacts

A small majority of entrepreneurs expect their venture capital partners to help in developing contacts within the industry.

Firms were asked about the areas where they sought help in developing connections. The firms which expected assistance in developing contacts indicated a broad variety of requirements. These firms identified, on average, more than two areas each where venture capitalists were expected to be able to provide industry connections. The industry contact most sought were business partners, followed by customers and alliance partners. Few firms felt that they needed assistance in locating suppliers.

The range of connections sought was broad, with no particular area being identified as significantly more important than another. Therefore, the broader the range of the venture capitalist's contacts, the greater is the chance that value added service can be provided to the investee firm.

Areas Where Connections Expected	% of Mentions
Business partners	31.7
Customers	29.3
Alliance partners	26.8
Suppliers	12.2
Total	100.0

Table 3.4 *Areas where entrepreneurs' seek help in developing industry connections*

The provision of second found finance

Prior discussion in Part Two highlighted the possibility that venture capitalists would often have to provide financing on more than one occasion. The survey revealed a preponderance of entrepreneurial firms who expected the venture capitalist to continue to provide finance when necessary.

These responses were cross tabulated with the stage of the respondent company's development. The result revealed that firms at an earlier stage of development were more inclined to expect continuing finance. Among start-up companies, 83% indicated that they expected further finance if necessary. This figure declined to 77% of early growth companies. Only one-third of growth firms indicated an expectation of continuing finance.

As enterprises mature their expectations for additional rounds of

Expectation of Continuing Finance	Start-Up %	Early-Growth %	Growth %
Yes	83	73	33
No	17	27	67
Total	100	100	100

Table 3.5 *Expectations concerning the supply of continuing finance stage of corporate development*

finance will diminish. Reasons for this are twofold:

- As firms mature, they are presumably experiencing an increase in sales revenues and internally generated cash flow. Thus, they will have less need for outside sources of finance;

- More mature firms may have greater access to alternative forms of finance, notably the credit market, once a track record has been developed.

Firms were also asked whether they expected venture capitalists to assist in obtaining further finance from other financiers. The survey revealed identical results to this question as to the preceding ones. The same proportion of respondents (22 out of 32) felt that, in addition to providing additional finance, the venture capitalist should assist in obtaining finance from other parties.

Selection criteria used by venture capital investees

The vast majority of entrepreneurs seeking venture capital finance will contact more than one venture capital firm. When asked how many venture capital firms they had approached and how many affirmative responses they had received, less than a quarter of the respondents indicated that they had contacted only one venture capital firm. Approximately one half had contacted between two and six. (Refer to Table 3.6.)

One enterprise had contacted 34 venture capital firms (offers of financing were forthcoming from four). Excluding that hopeful firm, the respondents to the survey indicated contacting an average of 5.5 venture capital suppliers.

In the majority of cases it turned out that, where a business plan appears attractive to one venture capitalist, it will be acceptable to at least one of his competitors. Of the 24 respondents who contacted more than one venture capitalist, the vast majority (75%) received offers of financing from more than one source.

The data generated from this survey suggests that the majority of successful entrepreneurs will contact a variety of sources, and where a business plan shows attractive attributes, these are usually recognised by more than one investor. Therefore, it can be inferred that a successful entrepreneur with a good business plan will have his choice of venture

Number Contacted	% of Mentions
1	22.6
2	3.2
3	12.9
4	9.7
5	3.2
6	19.4
7	0.0
8	6.4
9	0.0
10	9.7
more than 10	12.9
Total	100.0

Table 3.6 *Number of venture capitalists contacted*

Affirmative Responses	% of Mentions
1	25.0
2	25.0
3	12.5
4	20.8
5	12.5
6	4.2
Total	100.0

Table 3.7 *Number of affirmative responses for financing received*

capital providers, and that these latter are, to a large extent, chasing the same good propositions.

How to choose a venture capital firm

After having analysed the sort of advice and assistance entrepreneurs expect from their venture capitalist, we will now look at the attributes they seek in venture capital firms. What criteria does an entrepreneur faced with several financing offers use to make his choice? In the author's survey respondents were asked to choose from a list of ten attributes, those that they consider desirable in a venture capital firm. The ten attributes were grouped into three broad areas:

Intangible qualities or personal characteristics:

- Commitment to management/to the venture;
- Patience in receiving return on investment;
- Trustworthiness;
- Easiness to work with;
- Efficiency/speediness of response.

The venture capitalist's experience and track record:

- Reputation of the venture capitalist;
- Number of years of operation.

Financial considerations:

- Cost of raising finance;
- Possibility of buying back sold equity;
- Financial strength of the venture capitalist.

Two attributes were mentioned substantially more frequently than any other. *Commitment to management/to the venture* was identified in 26 of the 32 (81.3%) of the returned questionnaires. This was followed closely by *patience in receiving return on investment*, which received 24 mentions. Only one other attribute appeared in half or more of the questionnaires, *trustworthiness* was mentioned by exactly half of the 32 respondents.

At the other extreme, none of the 32 respondents attached any importance to the number of years that the venture capital firm had been in operation. Only 5 out of 32 (15%) considered financial strength to be important. (Refer to Table 3.8.)

Notably, four of the attributes considered by entrepreneurs to be most important related to intangible qualities and personal characteristics. Surprisingly, the cost of raising finance was viewed to be only the fourth most important attribute.

Note the rather clear preference for attributes which might fall under the general heading of the venture capital firm's *character* or *personality*, as opposed to its length of operation, its financial strength or its

Attribute	% of Surveys Mentioning
Commitment to management/to the venture	81.3
Patience in receiving return-on-investment	75.0
Trustworthiness	50.0
Cost of raising finance	43.8
Easiness to work with	40.6
Reputation of venture capitalist	34.4
Possibility of buying back equity	31.3
Efficiency/speediness of response	28.1
Financial strength of venture capitalist	15.6
Number of years of operation	00.0
Total number of surveys	100.0

Table 3.8 *Attributes sought in a venture capital firm*

reputation. This appears to confirm the opinion of venture capitalists themselves that personal chemistry is an essential element in the investor-investee relationship. It would also appear to be the corollary to the venture capitalists' maxim concerning investing in management, management, and management. Commitment, patience and trust are, to an entrepreneur, more notable hallmarks of a venture capitalist than track record, financial strength, efficiency or reputation.

Also notable is the fact that the cost of raising finance was identified to be a desirable attribute by less than half of the respondents. This would appear to confirm another maxim of the industry. That is, 'if the venture is a financial success there should be more than enough money for everyone'.

Interestingly, length of operation and reputation are not perceived as important by the majority of entrepreneurial firms. These two factors do therefore not pose barriers to entry on a newcomer to the industry. Commitment, patience and trust are seen as highly important, and may be seen as the key success factors within the industry.

Finally, entrepreneurs were asked to offer, unprompted, their selection criteria in choosing a venture capitalist. Thirteen respondents indicated that they had chosen one or more venture capitalists from out of larger field of potential investors.

Five chose strictly on the basis of terms of the offer. Reasons stated were: 'best terms', 'best price/terms', 'cost', 'offered cash, factory space and management' and 'cost of finance/profile of v.c.'.

Six chose on the basis of personality or character. Reasons stated were: 'ability to deliver', 'personality', 'speed and easiness to work with', 'trustworthiness', 'personality' (again), and 'those most likely to add value to business and be easy to work with'.

One chose for a combination of reasons: 'speed of response, efficiency/ flexibility, cost'. Finally, one entrepreneur offered the rationale 'first come, first served'.

It stands out that, where an entrepreneur has a choice between a number of willing investors, personality and character are given greater weight than financial conditions of the investment.

In view of the fact that venture capital firms seem, to a large extent, to be chasing the same good propositions, it is important for a venture capital firm to possess those attributes that successful entrepreneurs consider attractive: commitment to management, patience in receiving return on investment and trustworthiness.

12

Entrepreneur expectations and investor requirements: summary

This part of the book focused on the various forms of managerial assistance that firms seeking external equity will expect from a supplier of venture capital. It also served to identify those attributes which entrepreneurial firms seek in potential investors. Finally, the report identified some of the criteria, utilised by a sample of 32 UK firms, in selecting an appropriate venture capital investor.

The principal findings of the research were as follows:

- Entrepreneurs seeking outside capital have a high expectation of up-front advice. This expectation appears to decline as potential investees progress along their corporate development, (i.e. more mature firms feel less need for up-front advice).

- Entrepreneurs generally are expecting the venture capitalist to analyse the business idea, perfect the business plan, and validate the risk/reward ratio.

- The most needed forms of advice sought by entrepreneurs are of a financial and strategic nature.

- Generally, entrepreneurs expect a venture capitalist to be willing to supply more than one round of finance. This expectation appears to decrease (perhaps with a decreasing perception of need) with more mature companies.

- Entrepreneurs, irrespective of the stage at which they are seeking financing, expect their venture capital partner to assist in obtaining further financing from other sources.

- Entrepreneurs overwhelmingly accept the proposition that the venture capitalist must take a role in the direction of the company. The majority, however, prefer the venture capital investor to take an idea-sounding non-executive position at Board level.

- When asked to identify attributes seen as desirable in a venture capital investor, the survey's respondents identified attributes associated with the venture capitalists' character and intangible quantities. The three most important characteristics identified by investee firms were (i) commitment to management/to the venture (ii) patience in receiving return on investment and (iii) trustworthiness.

- The cost of raising finance was seen as the fourth most important attribute only. It was mentioned by less than half of the survey's respondents.

- The vast majority of entrepreneurial firms seeking financing approach more than one source. Those firms which are successful in attracting investment normally receive offers from more than one source.

- In choosing between competing offers of financing, entrepreneurs tend to place greater emphasis on the venture capitalist's qualities and characteristics than on the financial terms of any offer.

The above findings again seem to confirm the view held by venture capitalists themselves that venture capital investing is a people game and that personal chemistry is an essential requirement to making successful investments.

The fact that the majority of 'investible' propositions received more than one offer of financing would appear to confirm the notion within the industry that there is ample financing available for truly attractive deals.

Part four

The size and structure of the UK venture capital industry

13

The size and structure of the UK venture capital industry: introduction

In Part one, a definition of venture capital was offered. In Part two, consideration was given to the seven stages of venture capital funding. Part three examined the qualities and attributes that venture capital investors seek in potential investees, and vice versa. Part four, entitled 'The Size and Structure of the UK Venture Capital Industry' now turns its attention to the actual state of the industry in the UK in 1989.

The purpose of Part four is threefold:

- provide a brief statistical history of the growth and development of the UK venture capital industry;

- provide a statistical description of the industry as it now appears;

- identify current industry characteristics and trends.

After completing Part four the reader will know:

- the number of venture capital firms an entrepreneur can contact;

- where these venture capitalists get their funds;

- the volume of funds available for investment;

- the volume of activity by number and value of investments;

- investment by stage of company development;

- investment by country and region;

- investment by industry sector.

Part four contains material which is largely quantitative in nature. The majority of the data used are drawn from one of the following sources:

Venture Capital in Europe 1989 by Peat Marwick McLintock, on behalf of the European Venture Capital Association.

Report on Investment Activity 1988 by the British Venture Capital Association (BVCA).

Report on Investment Activity 1986 and 1987 by the BVCA.

Survey of the Impact of Venture Capital Arthur Andersen & Co. on behalf of the British Venture Capital Association, March 1987.

For further detail, the reader is encouraged to consult these publications directly, each of which is available from either the BVCA or the EVCA.

14

The UK venture capital industry

Some statistics

Despite its relatively recent origins, by 1987 the UK venture capital industry was the second largest in the world. While perhaps a quarter the size of the industry in the United States (where venture capital investment has its origins), the venture capital pool in the UK is 90% larger than that of the third-ranked country, Japan. (Refer to Table 4.1.)

Country	Total Number of Firms 1986	1987	Total Pool of Funds (£m)	(£m)
United States	550	530	13 900	15 500
United Kingdom	110	120	3 130	4 160
Japan	70	80	590	2 200
France	45	90	520	950
Canada	44	45	700	730
Netherlands	40	60	450	660
West Germany	25	30	350	440
Ireland	10	8	70	440
Italy	na	15	na	220
Sweden	31	30	225	150
Denmark	14	19	85	150
Norway	35	na	130	na
Spain	na	27	na	150
Belgium	na	10	na	150
Switzerland	na	15	na	75

Table 4.1 *Size of the international venture capital industry – 1986 and 1987 (Figures from Venture Economics)*

It may be remarkable that, among those countries with the most developed venture capital industries, the UK possesses substantially the largest pool of capital relative to the nation's GNP.

This suggests that, despite its relatively recent origins, the venture capital industry in the United Kingdom has quickly attained a highly developed state and forms an important part of the corporate finance community. Credit for this rapid growth can be given to a sympathetic combination of political, regulatory, fiscal, economic and investment factors.

(UK = 100)

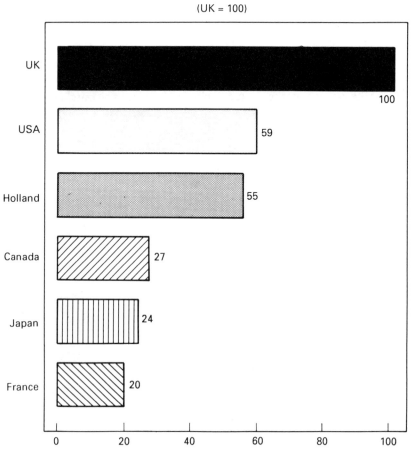

Figure 4.1 Leading countries' venture capital pools relative to GNP – 1987

Reasons for advanced position of the UK venture capital industry

Four reasons can be cited for the UK's relatively advanced position within the international venture capital scene:

- The political will to assist and support entrepreneurship and small business. In a recent speech by the Chairman of the British Venture Capital Association, he said 'We are fortunate, as a result of support from all political parties, to find the British venture capital industry in a stronger position than any other in Europe.'

- The UK is a nation of technicians. As Norman Fast, President of Venture Economics, (a US based venture capital consulting firm) observed in a speech to UK entrepreneurs: 'You [the UK] have the tremendous benefit of low cost engineering talent and labour ... you have high class technology and science coming out of the university system.'

- Ties with the US. The social, cultural, economic, and – perhaps most important – linguistic ties with the United States has made the UK more receptive to adopting a form of finance pioneered in that country.

- The UK's open economy, and London's role as the major centre of international finance and investment, has made it a welcome home to American practitioners seeking venture capital investment opportunities outside of their home market.

Venture capital industry organisations

The British Venture Capital Association

The British Venture Capital Association (BVCA) is the trade association for the UK's venture capital community. It is a lobbying and policy oriented grouping which acts on behalf of the common concerns of the industry's individual members. The stated objectives of the BVCA are:

- To act as a focus of members' views and interests in discussions with government, financial and regulatory authorities, and other trade or professional bodies;

- To provide a regular forum for the exchange of views among members, with the idea of encouraging joint investment participation in projects and of providing further stimulus to the UK venture capital industry; and

- To develop and maintain the highest standards of professional practice and ethics among member companies with substantial funds at their disposal for investment in venture capital projects.

Activities of the BVCA

Since 1985, the BVCA has published an Annual Report on Investment Activity, which presents aggregated data on the investment activity of BVCA member firms. The BVCA also publishes a quarterly newsletter, sponsors regional and London based conferences, co-sponsors an annual Venture Capital Forum in London as well as seminars and lectures aimed at professional development and liaison with the financial community. The BVCA plays no regulating or policing role in industry affairs.

Membership in the BVCA

Membership in the BVCA is open to professionally managed venture capital funds investing equity capital in return for minority equity stakes in unlisted companies. They may be independent funds or the venture capital arms of other organisations. As at April 1989 the BVCA reported 108 Full Members and 50 Associate Members (of which 7 were venture capital firms). Membership thus includes more than 70% of the total UK venture capital industry population.

The European Venture Capital Association

The European Venture Capital Association (EVCA) is the trade association and lobby group for the venture capital industry on a European scale. Founded in Brussels in November 1983, its stated aim is to:

> 'Provide for the examination and discussion of the management of and investment in venture capital in Europe ... with a view to developing and maintaining a venture capital industry as a means to providing equity finance for innovation and small and medium-sized enterprises, and to establishing high standards of business conduct and professional competence.' (From Venture Capital in Europe, EVCA, 1987).

Activities of the EVCA
One of the EVCA's activities is to establish a European Venture Capital Institute for the purposes of training and development of practising and young aspiring venture capital investors. A venture capital data base has been established to provide the member firms of the EVCA with rapid access to Europe-wide information on venture capital investment opportunities.

Membership in the EVCA
Beginning with 43 founding members, the EVCA's membership now includes 201 venture capital firms and related organisations in 23 countries. Membership is drawn from some of the largest venture investment firms operating in Europe, its associate membership is drawn from related professional organisations (banks, fund managers, accounting and consulting firms) as well as venture capital investment firms from outside of Europe. (Refer to Table 4.2.)

Full membership in the EVCA is open exclusively to organisations recognised as venture capital providers. These are defined as firms:

- which have a substantial activity in the management of equity or quasi-equity financing for the start-up and/or development of small

Country	Full Members	Assoc. Members	Total	Country	Full Members	Assoc. Members	Total
Belgium	11	9	20	Ireland	3	2	5
Switzerland	3	3	6	Israel	–	2	2
Canada	–	1	1	Italy	9	1	10
FR Germany	7	3	10	Luxembourg	1	2	3
Denmark	5	3	8	Netherlands	22	4	26
Spain	6	4	10	Norway	1	–	1
France	21	3	24	USA	–	6	6
UK	35	11	46	Portugal	4	4	8
Greece	–	2	2	Argentina	–	1	1
Iceland	–	3	3	Sweden	–	2	2
Finland	3	2	5	Japan	–	1	1
Austria	1	–	1				
				TOTAL	132	69	201

Table 4.2 *The European Venture Capital Association – membership distribution – 1987 (Figures from the EVCA)*

and medium sized enterprises that have a significant growth potential in terms of products, technology, business concepts and services;

● whose main objective is long-term capital gains to remunerate risks;

● who can provide active management support to investees.

The four-fold growth of EVCA membership over a period of four years reflects the growing internationalisation of the European venture capital industry, particularly with respect to cross-border investments and trans-national syndication of larger investments.

Number of venture capital firms

By the end of 1988 there were approximately 150 firms of varying sizes and investment orientations providing venture and development capital in the United Kingdom. Today's list of players exceeds by one-third the 113 venture capital firms reported at year end 1985. More remarkably, this number reflects a three and a half times increase in the size of the industry in just seven years.

Capital creation

In step with the increase in the number of sources of equity finance, the volume of funds being raised has shown a dramatic growth over the last decade. After an unprecedented decline in 1986, UK venture fund managers are surpassing all previous records for new capital raised for venture funds. In 1987 the BVCA member firms had raised a total of £708 million in new capital. This represents more than three times the amount raised in 1986. (Refer to Table 4.3.)

Sources of funds

In 1988 pension funds and insurance companies were the largest sources of venture capital funds, accounting for just over 64% of the total capital raised.

Industrial corporations still account for a comparatively low contribution to the pool of venture capital. This despite the increasing publicity being given to corporate venturing, a concept which is well known in the

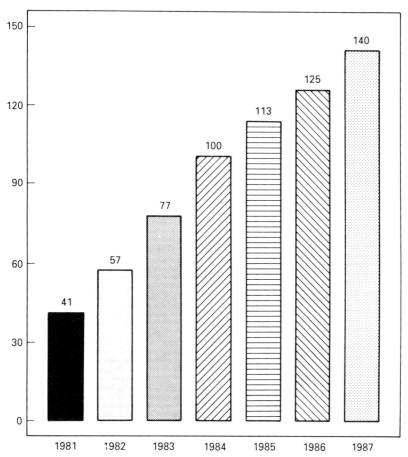

Figure 4.2 Venture capital investment firms in the UK – 1981–87

Type of Fund	1979 (£m)	1980 (£m)	1981 (£m)	1982 (£m)	1983 (£m)	1984 (£m)	1985 (£m)	1986 (£m)	1987 (£m)
Publicly listed	–	–	62.2	4.9	51.6	36.7	–	4.0	n/a
BSS and BES	–	–	9.8	4.2	44.6	37.5	31.3	26.5	n/a
Instit'ly backed	7.4	19.5	42.6	33.7	64.4	147.8	246.8	195.0	n/a
TOTAL	7.4	19.5	114.6	42.8	160.6	222.0	278.1	225.5	708.0

Table 4.3 New capital raised by British venture capital firms – 1979 to 1987
Note: These figures represent the 99 member firms of the BVCA only.
(Figures from Venture Economics)

United States but only recently beginning to gain acceptance in the UK. (Refer to Table 4.4.)

Volume of investment activity

The volume of investment activity of the BVCA's members is increasing dramatically, reflecting the growth of the industry. Between 1984 and 1988, the number of firms financed during each year by BVCA member firms more than trebled, increasing from 479 to 1529. The value of those investments increased more than seven times rising from £190 million to £1,394 million, surpassing the £1 billion plateau for the first time in 1988. (Refer to Table 4.5.)

Source	1987 (Ecu millions)	%	1988 (£ millions)	%
Pension Funds	560.8	19.0	756.3	21.7
Insurance Companies	360.6	12.2	408.7	11.7
Corporate Investors	477.7	16.1	290.1	8.3
Banks	1044.2	35.3	1080.3	31.0
Private Individuals	134.2	4.5	173.9	5.0
Government Agencies	112.0	3.8	169.8	4.9
Universities	16.8	0.6	4.3	0.2
Others	146.2	4.9	341.6	9.8
Retained Earnings	105.6	3.6	258.4	7.4
Total	2958.1	100.0	3483.4	100.0

Table 4.4   *Sources of funds for venture capital investment – UK – 1985 and 1986 (Figures from Peat Marwick McLintock)*

Year ending December 31	1984	1985	1986	1987	1988
Total investments – value (£mil.)	190	325	426	934	1394
Total investments – number	696	1021	1105	1726	2093
Average value of investment (£000)	273	318	385	541	957
Number of companies financed	479	635	708	1174	1527

Table 4.5   *Investment activity by member firms of the BVCA – 1984 to 1988 (Figures from the BVCA)*

15

Venture capital investments

Investment by syndication

Not only has the number of firms providing venture capital investment increased drastically, but the investments themselves are becoming larger, mainly through syndication. As with debt syndication, syndicated venture capital investment simply means the provision of finance to an investee through the pooling of funds of two or more separate investors. In 1988, the average venture capital investment in the UK attracted 1.37 investors. The established players now maintain rosters of potential syndicate partners with whom deals can be shared. The degree of syndication in the UK venture capital community probably reflects the growing maturity of the industry.

Benefits of syndication

The syndication of a venture capital investment provides a number of distinct benefits to both the investor and the entrepreneur. Of specific advantage to the investor are the following:

- Perhaps most important, syndication allows the spreading of investment risk, with each partner taking a smaller ownership position in a larger number of venture opportunities.

- Reciprocity between syndicate partners may also mean that deal flow can be maintained even when an individual venture firm may not be the originator of a deal.

Of mutual benefit to both the entrepreneur and the venture capitalist are:

- A larger number of investing firms will tend to improve the *due diligence* phase of the investment process, through the pooling of know-how and research capabilities, as well as through the contribution of the specific competencies of each.

- The inclusion of more than one investor creates the opportunity for greater valued-added to the investee through the contribution of the specific competencies of each venture capital firm.

- A wider investment syndicate will inevitably bring a wider range of business and finance contacts into the entrepreneurs' sphere.

- Because a larger number of investors are involved in the investment from the outset, syndication improves the opportunity for the entrepreneur to raise second or third round finance.

Growth of syndication

The trend toward increased syndication of investments (on a national more than on a trans-national basis) halted in 1988. The number of syndicated investments as a proportion of all venture investments rose from 58 to 72% between 1985 and 1987 but declined in 1988. (Refer to Table 4.6.)

Syndication: conclusions

Three conclusions are drawn with respect to the rising importance of

	1987		1988	
Syndication of Investments	(£000)	%	(£000)	%
No syndication	341,000	28.3	532,614	38.0
National syndication	813,000	67.5	831,369	59.3
Transnational syndication	50,000	4	38,017	2.7
TOTAL	1,204,000	100.0	1,402,000	100.0

Table 4.6 *Syndications as proportion of all venture capital investments UK – 1985 and 1986*
(Figures from the EVCA)

syndicated investment:

- Syndication is an increasingly characteristic aspect of venture capital investment in the UK.

- The syndication of investment opportunities within a small number of co-investors is a desirable thing from the point of view of both the investor and the entrepreneur.

- Scale (or more properly lack thereof) need not be a barrier to participation in larger financings where these will be sold down by syndicate leaders and managers to participants.

Investment by financing stage

Total investment by financing stage

The vast majority of UK venture capital investment is in the later stages of development, a trend which appears to be on the increase. Between them, expansion capital and MBO financings absorbed more than two-thirds (68%) of the funds invested in UK recipient firms in 1988.

Development or expansion capital accounted for the largest proportion, by number, of financings in 1988. Expansion financings declined slightly compared with the previous year and now represent just less than half (47.1%) of the total of all venture capital investments in the UK. By

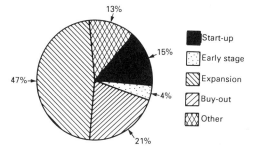

Figure 4.3a Total venture capital investment by financing stage (UK – 1988). Number of financings. (Figures from the BVCA)

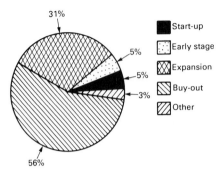

31%

5%

5%

3%

56%

Start-up

Early stage

Expansion

Buy-out

Other

Figure 4.3b Total venture capital investment by financing stage (UK – 1988). Value of investments. (Figures from the BVCA)

contrast, management buy-outs showed an increase from 16.5% in 1987 to 20.8% of the total number of venture capital financings in 1988.

Noteworthy are the differences between the percentage of total financings represented by each stage of investment and the percentage of the total amount of funding that each stage received. (Refer to Table 4.7.)

MBO financings, which accounted for some 21% of all financings, involved more than half of the total funds provided. The average MBO involved just over £2.6 million versus an average investment (all stages) of just £957,000.

Three reasons may be given for the paucity of seed capital investment and the high value associated with buy-outs:

- As the earliest stage of investment, it is also the least liquid, discouraging all but the most long term oriented and highly liquid investors.

- Perhaps no stage of a company's life will be more difficult to manage than the transition from prototype to start-up. The reluctance to invest in seed capital most probably reflects the feeling on the part of most venture capitalists that the risk/return trade-off is excessively weighted toward risk at this stage of company development.

- The short turn around between investment and realisation makes MBOs a particularly attractive investment in a bull market. The initial placement market was highly receptive during the mid 1980s, rendering MBOs both liquid and profitable.

Stage	Number of Investments			Percentage of Investments		
	1986	1987	1988	1986	1987	1988
Start-up	166	267	251	17.3	15.5	13.2
Early Stage	108	191	230	11.2	11.1	12.1
Expansion	359	806	788	37.3	46.7	41.5
Buy-out/buy-in	284	392	545	29.5	22.7	28.7
Other	45	70	85	4.7	4.0	4.5
TOTAL	962	1726	1899	100.0	100.0	100.0

Stage	Investments per Financing			Average Financing Size		
	1986	1987	1988	1986	1987	1988
Start-up	1.5	1.40	1.24	512	393	347
Early Stage	1.4	1.44	1.26	371	341	330
Expansion	1.3	1.28	1.23	362	436	629
Buy-out/buy-in	2.2	1.81	1.93	1,325	2,364	2,600
Other	1.6	1.94	1.67	725	702	647
TOTAL	1.5	1.43	1.40	605	773	957

Table 4.7 Average investment size by stage of company development – 1986 to 1988 (Figures from BVCA)

Investment by country

Despite efforts on the part of organisations such as the European Venture Capital Association, venture capital investment remains a fairly parochial business. While the volume of trans-border syndications may be on the increase as venture capital firms begin to develop contacts between themselves, there appears to be no notable willingness by UK venture capitalists to invest outside local markets.

Of the investments referred to above some 87% by number, representing 93% by value, went to companies located in the United Kingdom. The bulk of the remainder went to the United States. (Refer to Table 4.8.)

The BVCA data notably shows that external investment remained virtually unchanged (from £95 million to £96 million), a decline in real terms from 1987 to 1988. The unchanged volume was due to a

	Companies Financed			% Financed			Amount Invested (in £m)			% of Value		
	1986	1987	1988	86	87	88	1986	1987	1988	86	87	88
UK	600	1174	1326	85	91	87	384	934	1298	90	91	93
USA	95	103	137	13	8	9	37	83	41	9	8	3
Europe	11	21	38	2	2	2	5	12	47	1	1	3
Other	2	—	26	—	—	2	—	—	8	—	—	1
TOTAL	708	1298	1527	100	100	100	426	1029	1394	100	100	100

Table 4.8 *Distribution of venture capital investment by country – 1986 to 1988* (*Figures from BVCA*)

Year end December 31,	1984	1985	1986	1987	1988
UNITED KINGDOM					
Value of investments (£million)	139	278	384	934	1298
Companies financed	n/a	517	600	1174	1326
Average value (£000's)	n/a	537	640	796	978
NON-UK INVESTMENTS					
Value of investments (£million)	51	47	42	95	96
Companies financed	n/a	118	108	124	201
Average value (£000's)	n/a	398	388	774	478

Table 4.9 *Comparison of UK versus non-UK investment – 1984 to 1988* (*Figures from the BVCA*)

significantly smaller average non-UK investment in 1988 when compared to the prior year. (Refer to Table 4.9.)

Investment by country: conclusion

It is particularly interesting that the relative importance of external investment has declined during the past three years, even as organisations such as the EVCA have flourished, and the majority of financial institutions (banks, merchant banks, equity exchanges) have raised their international profile. Venture capital may be more problematic than other forms of investment, with its emphasis on hands-on involvement.

This overwhelming emphasis on domestic investments suggests that:

- The pro-active and participatory nature of venture capital investment requires that the investor and the investee be in reasonably close physical proximity to each other.

- The value-added nature of venture investment requires that the investor and the investee communicate in the same language.

- The complexity of international tax legislation, varying degrees of public sector control over private enterprise, differences in accounting and disclosure standards, etc. all weigh against the international venture capital investment.

With the imminence of a single European market for all goods and services in 1992, it is felt that venture capital investment will, in due time, increase its international dimension. However, it is not foreseen that this will happen via direct investment. It seems more likely that there will be a growth of international venture capital pools, funded by syndicates of venture firms in a variety of countries, and managed by the local partner in each locale.

Investment by region

Of UK companies financed by BVCA members in 1988, 80% were located in England. These companies received more than 90% of the funds invested. (Refer to Table 4.10.)

Of the companies financed by BVCA members during 1988 38% were located in Greater London or the South East. These companies received half of the total amount invested. Average amount invested per company in the South East was significantly higher than the UK national average (£1,186,700 versus £957,000).

The hands-on management style necessary for successful venture management requires that the venture capitalist be in close physical proximity to the investee. Regular meetings and discussions, whether formal (i.e. at Board level) or informal, are an important aspect of a successful investor-entrepreneur relationship.

While there appears to be no reluctance to invest in the regions, there exists a lack of sizeable venture capital projects. Although it might be supposed that there is a reluctance to commit relatively larger sums to the

Geographic Region	Number of Companies Financed		% of Companies Financed		Amount Invested (£m)		% of Amount Invested	
	1988	1987	1988	1987	1988	1987	1988	1987
South East								
North of Thames	176	116	13	10	97	63	8	7
South of Thames	70	138	5	12	178	177	14	19
Greater London	263	232	20	20	365	289	28	31
South West	78	74	6	6	53	67	4	7
West Midlands	119	86	9	7	119	40	9	4
East Anglia	60	68	5	6	38	24	3	3
East Midlands	72	75	5	6	86	71	7	8
Yorks & Humberside	36	70	3	6	80	68	6	7
North West	94	78	7	7	57	36	4	4
North	98	38	7	3	103	6	8	1
Scotland	145	116	11	10	81	50	6	5
Wales	94	71	7	6	27	42	2	4
Northern Ireland	21	12	2	1	14	1	1	—
TOTAL	1326	1174	100	100	1298	934	100	100

Table 4.10 *Distribution of venture capital investment by region – 1987 and 1988 (Figures from the BVCA)*

provinces, it is inferred that the smaller average investment per deal reflects a heavier component of leveraged buy-out and management buy-out activity, with their greater capital requirements, in the South East.

Two of the factors which may explain the differences in the size of capital committed to venture capital investments in the regions are:

- *Higher overhead*, particularly staffing, and other costs are faced by venture capital suppliers based in the South East, particularly London. All venture proposals, regardless of size, require the same amount of management time and effort. Thus, London and South-East based venture capital firms, with a greater propensity to invest in their local region, will be constrained to consider larger propositions only.

- *High geographic concentration of capital intense investees* (e.g. high technology, bio-medical, and computer related firms) requiring relatively large amounts of finance in London and the South-East. The heavy geographic concentration of these firms can be attributed to their proximity to

- Sources of product/technological innovation and research and development (e.g. the Oxbridge Universities).

- Concentration of the markets for these products or technologies.

- Concentration of sources of finance in London.

Investment by industry sector

Despite venture capital's popular image as being specialty finance for high technology and computer related industry, recent experience shows that this is not the case in the United Kingdom.

Consumer related businesses headed the list of investee companies, representing 23% of the investee firms in the BVCA's 1988 portfolio. consumer products was the largest sector in terms of funds received for the fourth successive year. (Refer to Tables 4.11 and 4.12). The predominance of consumer related investee companies represents a continuation of a pattern begun in 1984.

Sector	No. of Companies Financed				% of Companies Financed			
	1985	1986	1987	1988	1985	1986	1987	1988
Consumer Related	96	112	259	305	23	25	20	23
Computer Related	71	64	117	127	17	18	10	10
Electronics Related	39	35	73	68	9	8	6	5
Medical/Health	16	32	58	52	4	7	5	4
Industrial Products	44	35	125	155	10	8	11	12
Communications	34	28	53	37	8	7	5	3
Energy and Mining	7	3	14	19	2	1	1	1
Transportation	20	23	53	62	5	5	5	5
Construction	19	9	55	58	5	2	5	4
Financial Services	14	24	36	126	3	6	3	9
Other Services	33	64	190	109	8	14	16	8
Other Manufacturing	31	24	141	208	3	5	12	16
TOTAL	424	453	1174	1326	100	100	100	100

Table 4.11 *Volume of investment by industry sector – 1985 to 1988*
(Figures from BVCA)

| | Value (£m) Invested | | | | % of Value Invested | | | |
	1985	1986	1987	1988	1985	1986	1987	1988
Consumer Related	34	39	260	457	20	20	28	35
Computer Related	33	21	46	56	19	11	5	4
Electronics Related	21	15	39	19	12	8	4	2
Medical/Health	7	18	46	23	4	9	5	2
Industrial Products	12	13	101	103	7	7	11	8
Communications	13	14	17	18	8	8	2	1
Energy and Mining	2	1	8	6	1	1	1	—
Transportation	6	16	36	40	3	8	4	3
Construction	6	4	46	84	4	2	5	6
Financial Services	10	20	46	166	6	10	5	13
Other Services	15	25	218	72	9	13	23	6
Other Manufacturing	14	6	70	254	8	3	8	20
TOTAL	171	190	934	1298	100	100	100	100

Table 4.12 *Investment by industry sector – value of investment – 1985 to 1988*
(Figures from BVCA)

Computer and computer related investments continued their decline in terms of both number of companies financed and the total amount of investment. In 1988 investments show a proportional decline from 10.0% to 9.6% and in value from 4.9% to 4.3% of the total.

The disastrous performance of small unlisted electronics companies over the past three or four years has led to a significant decline (from 12.1% to 1.5% since 1985) in the proportional value of funds being directed toward this sector. This decline has been taken up by a significant flow of funds toward the industrial products sector and miscellaneous services. The continued slump in the North Sea oil industry explains an almost total lack of energy related venture capital finance provided in 1988.

Average investment by industry sector

The dominance of the consumer products sector in terms of total volume of investment and total investments made, is also reflected by average investment size which, in 1988, approached £1,500,000. (Refer to Table 4.13). By contrast, the average investment in the computer sector was

	Total Financings			Average Investment (£000s)		
	1986	1987	1988	1986	1987	1988
Consumer Related	112	259	305	346	1003	1498
Computer Related	64	117	127	336	391	440
Electronics Related	35	73	68	426	535	279
Medical/Health	28	58	52	547	786	442
Industrial Products	35	125	155	377	810	664
Communications	28	53	37	514	315	486
Energy and Mining	3	14	19	200	571	315
Transportation	23	53	62	674	687	645
Construction	9	55	58	389	840	1448
Financial Services	24	36	126	775	1283	1317
Other Services	64	190	109	397	1149	660
Other Manufacturing	24	141	208	258	498	1221
TOTAL	453	1174	1326	420	796	979

Table 4.13 *Average venture capital investment by industry sector in the UK – 1986 to 1988*
(Figures from BVCA)

just £440,000 (less than one half of the venture capital industry average) and in the electronics sector £279,000 (less than one third the industry average).

The industry sector which has received the highest average investment during three of the last four years has been financial services. In 1988 the average investment into this sector was £1.44 million, 50% higher than the industry average, and for the first time since 1985 just slightly less than the consumer products sector. This probably reflects the belief on the part of many venture capital investors that the financial services sector offers some of the more attractive growth opportunities to be had.

While technology oriented investor specialists, such as Hambro Advanced Technologies Trust, Murray Technology, British Technology Group, and Baillie Gifford Technologies may continue to find opportunities in their chosen sectors, the empirical evidence of recent UK venture investment suggests a pronounced and continuing trend away from computer related, electronic related, and other technology related investments.

16

Summary

The purpose of this part of the book was to provide a description of the actual state of the venture capital investment industry in the UK as it is at present.

In the discussion of the size of the industry, both in absolute and relative terms, it appears that there is no doubt venture capital is a large and growing factor in the world of corporate finance. With some £2.8 billion invested during the past three years, the UK venture capital pool represents the second largest such pool in the world, second only to the USA. In relative terms, the UK venture capital sector is nearly twice as large as that of the USA (relative to GNP) and four times as large as that of Japan.

The industry is structured around both domestic and trans-European venture capital associations which act as industry associations, lobby groups and forums for syndication, information and networking. The domestic association, the BVCA, claims the membership of some three quarters of the industry's participants, including all of the largest players. The BVCA continues to grow as more venture capital firms enter the market.

The one word which best describes the industry trend is growth. During the past decade in particular, the UK venture capital industry has experienced growth in terms of:

- the number of suppliers;

- the capital at their disposal;

- the number of companies financed;

- the average size of each financing;

- the number of participants per financing thanks to the increased tendency to syndicate investments.

It is foreseen that the consequence of this growth will be increasing specialisation by individual venture firms into market niches where experience or expertise give them an advantage. Portfolio diversification can be maintained through participation in investment syndicates.

In the discussion of characteristics of the UK venture capital industry, four principal themes emerged:

- The relative maturity of the industry and the large number of players has led to a high proportion of venture capital investment being syndicated. This was seen to have a variety of advantages to both investor and investee.

- Middle and later stage investments were seen to be the principal recipients of venture capital, particularly management buy-outs. These latter require significantly larger amounts of capital per deal than other forms of venture financing. Seed and start-up investments are not especially popular among the UK's suppliers of capital. The management buy-in, while increasingly publicised in the pages of the financial press, is only rarely seen.

- Despite the efforts of the EVCA, venture investment continues to be a highly parochial enterprise. Venture investments were seen to be local not only in terms of country, but also in terms of region.

- Despite its reputation as a supplier of finance to high technology firms, both the statistical evidence of recent venture capital investment and the comments of practitioners lead to the conclusion that there will continue to be a swing away from investment involving new technology or high technology.

The industry's growth during the past decade has been notable. The growth and development of the UK venture capital industry are largely due to a sympathetic environment and to the emergence of market opportunities.

Part five

The current environment and market opportunity

17

The current environment and market opportunity: introduction

Development of the UK venture capital industry in the late 1970s

One of the main distinctions between the venture capital industry of the UK and that of the US, where the venture capital investment business has its origins, is that of maturity. The United States' private venture capital industry has been in existence for some thirty years.

In the UK, however, until the mid-1970s the industry was dominated by a small number of pioneers and specialists. An established market for professionally raised and invested pools of equity capital for entre-preneurial firms was limited. The provision of equity capital for many years had been the almost exclusive province of entrepreneurs (in the case of private companies) and the London Stock Exchange (in the case of public companies). The number of professionally managed venture capital companies in operation at the end of the 1970s was about a dozen.

Reasons for late development

The relatively late development of the venture capital industry in the UK vis-a-vis North America is attributed to a number of sources:

- The UK suffered from an anti-business, anti-enterprise culture. '...Business was considered both socially and academically infra-dig and young people were advised to join the professions or to become academics or civil servants.'

- High marginal rates of income tax, and the existence of death taxes reduced the amount of investible capital held by the personal sector, often the likely source of high risk start-up and development capital.

- The reluctance on the part of the UK's Clearing Banks to provide term finance to firms in search of growth capital. This was one of the principal conclusions of the Wilson Report on the financing of British industry.

Recent growth

It is only since the mid-1970s that the UK venture capital community has been an industry of any substance, with more than just a few isolated players. As recently as 1975, the industry contained only a dozen firms. (Refer to Table 5.1) In 1988, venture capital finance was available from some 140 sources.

Causes of growth

The rapid growth of the UK venture capital industry during the past decade has been brought about by a combination of structural, political, social, fiscal, economic, and investment factors which remain intact today. This suggests that venture capital investment is a phenomenon which will continue to grow in the 1990s.

	1952	1975	1979	1984
Clearing Bank Related Institutionally Backed	1	3	5	13
Captive/Semi-captive	1	3	5	27
Independents	—	3	6	30
BSS/BES funds	—	—	—	30
Corporate/Academic/Other	—	2	3	6
Semi-state Bodies	—	1	4	10
Total	2	12	23	116

Table 5.1 *UK venture capital fund management groups – 1952 to 1984*
Source: Venture Capital Today, Tony Lorenz.

Purpose of Part five

The purpose of part five is twofold:

- identify all those elements which have contributed to the recent and dramatic growth of the venture capital investment industry in the UK;

- identify factors which suggest a continuing market opportunity for both investors and entrepreneurial firms to benefit from this growing industry.

Structure of Part five

Part five identifies four broad areas, and considers what effect each has had upon the environment for venture capital investment in the United Kingdom. The areas identified are:

- fundamental changes in the structure of the economy;

- changes in the social and political environment;

- changes in the fiscal environment;

- changes in the economic environment.

The text then devotes a chapter to the investment markets, in particular those markets most likely to impact on the venture capitalist's ability to realise on his investment. These are the junior tiers of the regulated stock exchange and its unregulated competitors, namely the Unlisted Securities Market, the Third Market and the Over-the-Counter market.

Finally, a chapter is devoted to the Business Expansion Scheme, and the role which it has played in 'the current environment and market opportunity' for venture capital investing in the UK.

18

The current environment for venture capital investing

Fundamental changes in the structure of the UK economy

The maturing of the UK economy has led to fundamental changes in its structure. The emphasis has moved from producing physical goods to providing information and services and this has had its impact on various sectors.

Decline in the heavy industry sector – UK

The traditional, smokestack manufacturing industries, the industries which dominated the UK economies during the first half of the twentieth century show a decline in the number of employment positions they offer (both relative to other sectors and absolutely). Such labour and capital intensive industries as mining, ship building, textiles and engineering have been net losers of jobs over the past decade and a half. (Refer to Table 5.2.) Their place in the job creation role of the UK economy has been taken instead by a large number of service and technology based companies.

Growth in small firm sector

A second structural change has been the decline in the proportion of workers employed in medium sized or large firms, versus the increase in the number of workers employed by small businesses. (Refer to Table 5.3.)

While the number of medium and large sized manufacturing companies declined by 0.6% during the period 1975–1980, the number of small manufacturing firms increased by 0.2%.

More notable is that, while employment in large manufacturing industries decreased by 0.6% annually and in medium sized manufac-

| | ('000 of employees) | | | % change |
	1971	1981	1986	1971–86
Total Employees	22122	21870	21594	− 2.38
Agriculture, Forestry, Fishing	432	352	329	− 23.84
Metal, Engineering, Vehicles	3705	2919	2335	− 36.97
Energy, Water, Coal Mining	797	709	539	− 32.34
Mineral and Ore Extraction	1278	934	778	− 39.12
Other Manufacturing	3102	2367	2126	− 31.46
Construction	1207	1138	992	− 17.81
Distribution, Hotels, Catering	3678	4166	4403	+ 19.71
Transport & Communication	1150	1423	1341	+ 16.61
Banking, Finance, Insurance	1336	1740	2203	+ 64.90
Other Services	5036	6121	6548	+ 30.02

Table 5.2 *Employees in employment by industry in the UK – 1971 to 1986* (Figures from HMSO)

	Small (1–99)	Medium (100–449)	Large (500+)
MANUFACTURING SECTOR			
Number as % of all firms	94%	4%	2%
% of annual change 1975–80	+0.2%	−3.5%	−2.9%
Employment as % of all jobs	19%	13%	68%
% annual change 1975–1980	+2.2%	+0.1%	−0.6%
SERVICE SECTOR			
Number as % of all firms	99%	1%	—
Employment as % of all jobs	(45%)	(5%)	(50%)

Table 5.3 *Employment in small and medium sized firms – 1975 to 1980* (Figures from the Economics Intelligence Unit)

turing firms grew by 0.1%, employment in the small (less than 99 employees) manufacturing sector grew at a rate of 2.2% per year. The *Financial Times* reported during the spring of 1989 that 96% of all businesses in the UK employ fewer than 200 people. They provide 35% of all private sector jobs and 20% of business turnover.

Increase in number of business enterprises

A third structural change is an absolute rise in the number of businesses. The total number of business enterprises in the United Kingdom stood at just over half a million in 1970. This number increased to over one million in 1985. More significantly, the number of new company registrations tripled from 30,000 in 1970 to 100,000 in 1985. The number of business start-ups in the UK is now at record levels. New VAT registrations had reached 1400 per month by the spring of 1989, double the level for the decade of the 1980s as a whole.

Increase in number of self employed

In conjunction with the above, there has been a growth in the number of self employed. While the number of employees in the UK fell by 2.5% during the period 1971 to 1986, the number of self employed increased by nearly 30% (Refer to Table 5.4.)

	1971	1981	1986	% change 1971–86
Manufacturing	131	148	211	+ 61.1
Services	1231	1298	1646	+ 33.7
Agriculture	314	276	274	− 12.7
Construction	351	396	495	+ 41.0
Other	—	1	1	—
TOTAL	2026	2119	2627	+ 29.7

Table 5.4 *Total number of self-employed in the UK –*
1971 to 1986
(Figures from HMSO)

Fundamental changes in the structure of the UK economy and venture capital: conclusions

The increase in the number of small (often owner operated) flexible, service or information oriented, low capital base companies during the past decade has co-incided with – or was perhaps causal to – the growth in the supply of UK venture capital. If the social, political, economic, fiscal, and investment climates are propitious, one may expect to see a continued growth in the number of businesses which display the above characteristics, and which are ideally suited for venture capital finance as opposed to conventional debt finance.

Improved climate for small business and entrepreneurship

In tune with this change in the structure of UK industry there has been a change in the variety of, and attitudes toward, the financing of business in general and small business in particular. A recent survey of the small business sector in the *Financial Times* concludes that the climate for small business is changing for the better as the general wave of enthusiasm for the economic virtues of entrepreneurship begins to produce concrete results. Recognition of the role of small enterprise and new business has come from all sectors. Private sector organisations including the Clearing Banks provide a wider range of information and advisory services specifically geared toward the small, new or emerging business sector. The foremost examples thereof are the Loan Guarantee Scheme and the European Coal and Steel Community loan schemes for which most clearing banks act as agents and providers of funds. Leading this change of attitudes have been the Bank of England and the government itself.

Leading role taken by the Government

Recognising the particular needs of small, information or technology based businesses the Government has been one of the leaders in creating an environment sympathetic to small business and sympathetic to investment and finance. Much of this concern for small business was displayed in the Bolton Report, and for the financing of business in the

Wilson Report. Indeed, some have claimed that the development of the UK venture capital industry is the financial sector's response to the Wilson Report.

State-backed schemes encourage lending institutions to provide debt capital to the small firms sector. The foremost example of these is the Loan Guarantee Scheme, a scheme whereby government guarantees are provided to lenders to small and emerging businesses.

Other state-backed schemes are, for example, the Enterprise Allowance Scheme, which provides subsistence income to unemployed people who want to start up business, and the Enterprise Initiative, which provides subsidised management consultancy advice to existing small firms.

The government has also helped to stimulate private business development through a series of general programmes designed to provide both infrastructure and funding directly through:

- regional development grants;

- enterprise zones;

- science parks;

- low interest loans.

More selective aid is directed to rural areas, new towns, inner-city areas, and areas hard hit by redundancy in the steel industry.

This attitude of promoting the growth and development of private, especially small, business is perhaps not surprising given the generally free-market and enterprise philosophy of the present government. However, official concern for and support of the small business sector goes back to before the election of the Tories in 1979. It also extends beyond Whitehall to Threadneedle Street, where the Bank of England has long been one of the principal advocates for the provision of long term finance.

The prevailing economic creed of the 1960s was to put faith into big business to produce income and employment. As the Bank of England, in its submission to the Wilson Committee, noted:

'...For some 15 or 20 years prior to the present decade [written in 1978], the financing of industry and commerce proceeded without difficulty within the financial system whose structure was described in the Radcliffe Report of 1959. Industrial and commercial profitability did not appear to place a limit on the scale of new investment, and the external financing requirement of companies in the private sector was met by the banking system and capital market without problems of any severity arising.' (From: *Written Evidence of the Bank of England, Volume 5, Evidence on the Financing of Industry and Trade, Committee to Review the Functioning of the Financial Institutions.*)

However, throughout the 1970s it became apparent that big business was simply failing to deliver. Large firms failed not only to provide jobs; in many cases they failed even to maintain them. The Bank of England, in attributing causes to this failure, pointed to the apparent disinclination among banks and institutional shareholders to concern themselves with the causes of managerial failure in the companies in which they had financial interests, and the disinclination of investors (both debt and equity investors) to seek remedies as distinct from cutting losses.

Leading role taken by the Bank of England

The Bank of England, as maker of banking policy and arbiter of banking practice, identified the arm's length and re-active (as opposed to pro-active) approach to corporate finance, as one of the principal causes of corporate decline in the UK in the 1970s:

'It was argued that the conventional relationship between finance and industry in the United Kingdom, at least as regards medium and large companies, was too "arm's length". Institutional shareholders, whose importance had been growing for some years, were said to regard the sale of shares through the market as the only appropriate course when an investment looked like deteriorating. Direct action to remedy the situation in the company concerned in concert with the other large shareholders, or with major creditors, was not a familiar course. Analogously, it appeared that the operation of the established overdraft system of bank lending did not in practice enable the banks to acquire a flow of information about their customers' affairs such as might enable them to bring beneficial influence to bear upon boards and managements at a sufficiently early stage. There was some doubt indeed as to whether either the banks or the institutional shareholders had the capacity to identify the causes of impending failures, or to decide on appropriate remedies.' (From: *Written Evidence of the Bank of England, Vol. 5, Evidence on the Financing of Industry and Trade*)

Leading by example, the Bank of England is one of the larger shareholders (15.0%) in Investors in Industry plc, one of the world's largest, and the UK's oldest, venture capital companies.

In 1976, the Bank used its position to encourage and assist in the creation of Equity Capital for Industry (ECI), the venture capital management arm for a consortium of some 300 life insurance and pension fund investors.

With the active sponsorship and endorsement of the Bank of England and with the active support of a pro-business, pro-investment government, the market environment has been well disposed to venture capital investment.

Changes in the fiscal environment

Direct aid by way of loans and grants is the first and most apparent way in which the central government can give financial assistance to the small firm and growth business sectors. Less direct financial aid comes by way of fiscal measures.

A non-exhaustive list of taxation measures implemented within the last several years would include:

- *State-subsidised incentive schemes* to channel private equity investment into the small business sector. Foremost among these is the Business Expansion Scheme, a scheme which entails generous tax concessions to private investors putting equity into certain types of unlisted private companies. In addition, there is the Venture Capital Scheme which, like its more high profile counterpart, seeks to encourage equity investment in unquoted companies through the granting of tax relief (to both individuals and corporations) which can be claimed at the highest rate of tax on capital losses incurred.

- *Reduced rates of corporation tax* for firms earning below £500,000 in profits. The government has reduced the small firms' basic rate of tax three times from 31% to 29% to 27% and now to 25%.

- A similar *reduction in the basic rate of personal income tax*, from 31% to 25%. In addition, the highest marginal rate of personal income tax has been reduced from 83% to 60% and now to 40%. This lowering of personal tax rates has had the effect of putting more disposable income into the hands of entrepreneurs and independent businessmen. It has also had the effect of removing some of the disencentive toward financial success.

- *The passage of certain provisions in the Companies Act (1986)* allowing companies to buy back their own shares. This recognised the difficulties faced by small unquoted companies in raising equity capital. An entrepreneur might otherwise have been reluctant to sell an interest in his company if it was felt that he had no means of repurchasing that interest. Similarly, an investor might be reluctant to be locked into the shares of an unquoted or narrowly traded company if it felt that share repurchase were an option outside of the entrepreneur's reach. Tax relief is granted on interest incurred for share repurchase.

Not all fiscal measures implemented during the past decade have necessarily been beneficial to venture capital investing specifically, or indeed to long term equity investment generally. On the deleterious side are:

- The removal of the preferential tax treatment of capital gains, putting them on the same footing for taxation purposes as current income. This has had the effect of removing some of the advantages of investing long term for capital gain, and may cause a widening of the 'equity gap' where early stage, longer term venture opportunities are concerned.

- The lowering of the top marginal rate of tax, while freeing up disposable income for all manner of consumption and investment, has lowered some of the tax benefits of BES investing.

Notwithstanding that there have been some measures which may have harmed the climate for venture capital investing, the majority of fiscal measures instituted by the current government have created a taxation environment conducive to long term equity investment. While the current opposition party has avowed to raise both personal and corporation taxes upon forming its next government, it is suggested that it will do so only at the peril of popular opinion. In any event, it is felt to be unlikely that the UK will return to the taxation levels of the late 1970s.

Changes in the economic environment

During the past decade, a number of factors have contributed to an improved macroeconomic climate for long term equity investment. Generally, the ten years of rule by a government with generally free market and free enterprise attitudes have been favourable. Specifically, the following elements of policy are worth nothing:

- *Falling Inflation.* Retail price inflation has fallen from more than 20% at its peak in 1980 to 4% in 1987 and is now expected to be 5–6% at the end of 1989.

- *Economic Growth.* In real terms, the economy has grown at an average rate of $3\frac{1}{2}$ per cent per year since 1983.

- *Declining PSBR.* The budget of 1988 calls for a net repayment of public sector debt. This represents only the second time since the early 1950s that there has been a budget surplus. The Government's medium term financial strategy calls for a PSBR of zero – a balanced budget.

The present political and fiscal environments, characterised by a strong majority in Parliament and declining personal and corporate taxes, are conducive to the provision of venture capital investment and the receptivity of entrepreneurs to this form of finance.

19

Changes in the investment market

Any discussion of the venture capital market must make due consideration of divestment media: the means of getting out. Venture capital financing activities will flourish only where investors have access to open and liquid securities markets which can serve as exit media, or sources of follow-on finance.

The UK domestic equity markets are either recognised (under the control of the Stock Exchange) or unrecognised (independent of the Stock Exchange). The three recognised markets are:

- the Listed Exchange;

- the Unlisted Securities Market (USM);

- the Third Market.

The unrecognised market is the Over-the-Counter market (the OTC).

Until the mid-1970s, once an entrepreneur had exhausted his private capital, he had few formal sources of equity finance beyond the Listed Exchange. The Listed Exchange was expensive, time consuming and difficult to enter. Likewise, the venture capitalist was probably stifled without the benefit of a variety of public equity markets which could serve as alternatives, complements, or exit media for his own investments. With the creation of the OTC in the early 1970s, and the subsequent creation of two lower tiers to the recognised Stock Exchange (the Unlisted Securities Market or USM and the Third Market), the opportunities for, and profile of, corporate finance by way of formal equity capital markets have been dramatically enhanced.

This chapter is therefore concerned with a discussion of the three youngest and smallest of the public equity markets:

- the USM;

- the Third Market;

- the OTC.

The Unlisted Securities Market

The USM was established by the Stock Exchange Council in November 1980, in order to provide access to the public equity capital markets for firms that were too young or too small to obtain a Full Listing.

Between November 1980 and May 1989 a total of 732 firms had entered the USM. As at May 1989, the USM was trading the shares of 416 companies. The balance had either merged or been acquired, gone out of business or, in the case of 132, graduated to a Full Listing.

The USM: entry requirements

The USM permits flotation of firms which are both younger and smaller than those traded on the Listed Exchange. The distribution of the equity

	USM	Full Listing
Trading Record	3 years	5 years
Minimum market capitalisation	No lower limit	£700,000
Minimum equity in public hands	10%	25%
Annual fees	£1,000	Up to approx. £3,500
Entry fees	Nil	Up to approx. £15,000
Advertising in national press	Placing: Box advert	Placing: Advert & prospectus
	Introduction: Advert	Intro: Advert and prospectus
	Offer for sale: More	Offer: Two full prospectuses
Accountants' reports	Only mandatory for offer for sale	Mandatory

Table 5.5 *Different requirements of the USM and Full Listing*

need be less wide and the cost (both direct and indirect) of obtaining USM quotation is less than that of the Listed Exchange. (Refer to Table 5.5.) Companies seeking to trade on the USM need to have:

- a trading record of three years, as opposed to five years for Full Listing;

- no minimum amount of market capitalisation, as opposed to £700,000 for Full Listing;

- only 10% of the equity in public hands, as opposed to 25% for Full Listing.

The USM: characteristics

The USM has broadened away from the traditional highly speculative penny stocks which were among the first to have sought USM listing – oil and high technology. These sectors today represent little more than 10% of the market, largely because of the eclectic nature of newer listings taken on during the last two or three years.

The declining value of the market capitalisation of the electronics and high technology sectors mirrors the declining interest in these sectors by the venture capital industry. Their spectacularly volatile share price history provides the reason why. In October 1984 the USM listed 33 companies in the electronics sector, having a total market capitalisation of £516 million. One year later the number of electronics firms had increased to 40, but their market value had fallen to £339 million, a decline of 34%. A similar experience has occurred in the computing sector where the nine computer hardware manufacturers listed on the USM dropped 61% in value during 1985, and the six computer distribution companies dropped some 37%.

Difficulties of going public via the USM

A 1987 study of the USM by Stoy Howard revealed that most firms moving to the public equity markets experience severe shock in their opening months as quoted firms. Eighty-two per cent of the 142 USM firms surveyed indicated that they had encountered significant post-flotation problems. Twelve per cent went so far as to say that the problems of going public outweighed the benefits. The problems most commonly cited were:

- increased public scrutiny and media interest – 61%

- increase in reporting requirements – 50%

- pressure to pay dividends – 39%.

These problems are the ones an entrepreneurial firm could expect although clearly the effects of going public are greater than most firms estimate. This suggests opportunities for venture capitalists to finance firms which are capable of accessing one of the public equity markets but, for some of the reasons cited above, are be reluctant to do so.

After just seven years in existence, the success of the USM has been such that the Stock Exchange saw fit to spawn an even more junior market, the Third Market. With the Third Market still in its infancy, however, the USM will continue to be the natural destination of private companies looking for public equity and for venture capitalists and entrepreneurs looking to reap capital gains on their successful investments. Many professional investors, such as venture capitalists, express concern over the liquidity and image of the Third Market and the OTC. Thus, the USM is expected to remain one of the primary exit windows of the UK venture capital industry.

The growing number of USM listings, and the broad range of corporations from all sectors suggest that the USM has attained both maturity and credibility among underwriters and investors alike, and this is a positive development in the realm of venture capital finance.

The Third Market

The Third Market was launched on 26 January 1987, and it is the lowest tier of the Stock Exchange. Its objective is to provide a disciplined market place for the securities of young, expanding companies and for those whose shares had previously been traded outside of the Stock Exchange. The Third Market is intended to fill the equity gap for firms which are:

- recently established, needing only a minimum of one year's trading activity and one year's audited accounts;

- not yet trading, but which can demonstrate a well researched business plan;

- currently trading their shares on the Over-the-Counter market (OTC) and shown to be suitably qualified to be offered to the public.

As at May 1989 there were 58 companies trading on the Third Market.

Entry requirements for the Third Market are significantly less onerous than for the USM, not only in terms of age and size of the company acceptable for flotation, but also in terms of complexity and cost of the various listing procedures.

Candidates for the Third Market must be UK incorporated firms and must have the sponsorship of a member firm of the Stock Exchange. Sponsorship implies the vetting of the business plan, and the responsibility for ensuring the suitability of a candidate firm. Otherwise, the principal distinctions between the USM and the Third Market are as shown below in Table 5.6.

The Stock Exchange will not accept companies for Third Market flotation which derive at least 10% of either their profit or turnover from:

- holding cash or near cash assets;

- holding minority interests in other companies (for example venture capital companies or management companies);

- property management or real estate development companies;

- commodity holding or dealing companies.

The proscription against these types of companies can be interpreted as having two bases. The Stock Exchange appears to be avoiding the flotation of companies which are highly speculative by their very nature, for example, real estate related firms or commodity dealers. Also, the

Entry Requirement	Third Market	USM
Minimum % Equity to be held by the public	No set minimum	10%
Minimum Trading Record	1 year (may be waived)	3 years
Maximum period since last audit	1 year (may be waived)	9 months

Table 5.6 *Requirements for firms seeking flotation on the Third Market and the USM*

Stock Exchange seems to show an active bias toward industrial and service type firms.

The Third Market: characteristics

Being the youngest and the smallest of the Stock Exchange's three markets, and the easiest to enter, the Third Market is typified as substantially riskier than either Full Listing or the USM. Companies listed on the Third Market are predominantly young and small themselves, so in many ways the market is a substitute or competitor to venture capital finance, as opposed to the USM, which plays the role of exit medium.

Typically, companies trading on the Third Market will have a turnover in the region of £4 million to £8 million. However, the range is from £1.6 million to £53 million.

Despite its apparent attractions as a means of raising or realising equity finance, the initial two years of the Third Market's existence can be typified by its slower than forecast growth. The total of 59 firms listed by the spring of 1989 pales in comparison with initial expectations of 200 or more by the market's first anniversary. This is probably not a reflection of failure, merely a slower growth pattern than expected. Reasons cited were:

- unrealistically optimistic expectations, inflated by the previous success of the Unlisted Securities Market;

- a reluctance of small firms to see themselves as guinea pigs;

- a wait-and-see attitude by sponsors;

- the October 1987 crash, with its dampening effect on the IPO market (five firms had expected to seek a Third Market placement in October 1987; in the face of Black Monday, only one did);

- the continued existence of the Over-the-Counter market. In the face of the Financial Services Act, the possible demise of the OTC was widely forecast. It was expected that many OTC firms would move to the Third Market. In the event, the Financial Services Act has been cumbersome to implement and efforts are afoot within the OTC to increase the quality of its regulation and supervision.

Third Market sponsors remain confident that interest in the Market is high. Quality, for the time being, is lacking. The perception among sponsors and brokers is that the quality of business plans and initial prospectuses will rise as the Market attains a higher profile. Typical comments are:

'applicants were of a mixed quality, often bad.'

'applicants are mainly rubbish, but at least there are many approaches.'

'it is better to ensure that the companies which join the Third Market are the right quality rather than let a flood of lesser quality companies join the market and ruin its reputation.'

The principal feature of the Third Market is that it can provide a relatively high profile and well regulated route by which small and growing companies can raise equity finance. It is significantly less costly than either the USM or Full Listing, yet can provide the firm seeking finance with more credibility and marketability than trading shares elsewhere.

In practice, the Third Market has suffered from a slow start, caused not by a lack of interest, but by a lack of knowledge on the part of entrepreneurs as to the expectations and requirements of the public market. In short, the current difficulties experienced by the Third Market create opportunities for the venture capital community.

The Over-the-Counter market

The UK Over-the-Counter (OTC) market was established in 1972 by the investment bankers Granville and Company. Their objective was to provide an alternative to the Stock Exchange, both for companies that wished to raise finance and for investors. The next company to engage in OTC trading was Harvard Securities Ltd, in 1973. This company aimed particularly at small expanding companies which required equity but failed to meet the stringent regulations stipulated by the Stock Exchange's Full Listing. At the time of the OTC market's emergence the USM and Third Market were, of course, not yet in existence.

Although growth was initially slow, the principle of share dealing outside of the Stock Exchange was firmly established. There are now over 200 companies which take advantage of the OTC facilities. In addition, there are now 15 companies which act as market makers in OTC shares.

The OTC: entry requirements

There are no formal obligations associated with entry to the OTC. Each market maker is responsible for establishing its own formal procedures for entry. Any prospectus will have to comply with the Companies Act 1985. It is usual for any marketing document prepared to meet the standard set by the Stock Exchange. Although these are the entry requirements which are now in effect, within the next few months there may well be large changes due to the enforcement of the rules of individual SROs under the terms of the Financial Services Act.

The cost of entry to the OTC markets typically ranges from £40,000 (for a placing raising £250,000) to £180,000 (for an offer for sale raising £3 million).

Since the introduction of the BES, the number of companies trading on the OTC has rapidly increased. Statistics show that one third of the companies floated on the OTC from 1983 to 1986 were also funded, at some stage, by the BES. It would appear, therefore, that the OTC provides an ideal trading place for venture capitalised firms which wish to raise additional equity. As with companies trading on the Third Market, companies trading Over the Counter are, for taxation purposes, classed as unquoted.

Regulation of the OTC

Apart from the Department of Trade and Industry's (DTI) control over the issue of licences, there is no formal mechanism at present for the regulating of the OTC. Therefore, the market's operation depends upon the 'integrity and efficiency of the firms and companies concerned' and not on any formal regulation other than the Licensed Dealer (Conduct of Business) Rules, 1983.

The reputation of the OTC rests firmly in the hands of the sponsoring market-makers. They must exercise caution and provide advisory service to both investors and companies wishing to trade their shares via this market. With the introduction of the Financial Services Act market makers on the OTC are now required to join one of the 5 SROs.

Negotiations are now underway between the OTC Practitioners Committee and the SIB.

Industry sectors

A recent listing of OTC companies identifies 208 firms using this market. The OTC is concentrated in four sectors, which together account for more than 44% of all of the traded firms. (Refer to Table 5.7.)

By contrast, these sectors account for just 20% of the firms traded on the recognised Stock Exchanges. Some have argued that the predominant sectors on the OTC (real estate speculation, oil and gas exploration) are intrinsically more risky than the industrial metal or investment management sectors which lead the Stock Exchange.

Reasons for trading OTC

Research was undertaken on the attitudes and perceptions of firms listed on the Over-the-Counter market. The research was intended to place the OTC within the equity capital spectrum as a substitute, complement, or exit medium for venture capital finance.

Entrepreneurs were asked to give their rationale for seeking outside finance. Fully 60% of the respondents identified company expansion or the financing of new developments as their rationale for raising capital via the OTC. (Refer to Table 5.8.)

Sector	Firms	%
Finance/Property	35	16.7
Leisure	26	12.7
Oils and Gases	17	8.1
Electricals/Electronics	14	6.7
4 Sector Concentration	92	44.2
Total – Classified by Sector	208	100.0

Table 5.7 *Sectoral concentration of firms trading over the counter – 1987*
(Figures from Hambro Company Guide 1987)

Rationale Given	% of Responses
Expansion	39
New Development	21
Improve Debt/Equity Ratio	12
Realise Some of Equity	14
Other	14

Table 5.8 *Reasons identified by companies for trading their shares on the OTC (Source: S. J. Smith)*

Responses listed under the heading of 'Other' included:

- to create a market for existing shareholders.

- to raise money for family members of firm.

- for taxation reasons, while the firm was under BES.

Options considered other than the OTC
When asked to identify some of the options considered by companies prior to trading on the OTC entrepreneurs most often identified private placement or venture capital. (Refer to Table 5.9.)

Other options considered included the possible sale of the firm to a third party or participation in the BES. It is concluded from this that the

Option Considered	Number of Responses	% of Responses
To raise debt	5	20
Third Market	2	8
USM or Full Listing	4	16
Private Equity/Venture Capital	11	44
Other	3	12

Table 5.9 *Options considered by companies other than raising equity via the OTC (Source: S. J. Smith)*

OTC is perceived by entrepreneurs as a substitute for venture capital finance.

When asked to identify the advantages and disadvantages of the OTC, those inherent to the firm and relative to the other capital markets (e.g. the Stock Exchange or venture capital), half of the respondents identified *ease of entry* as the OTC's primary feature. It was felt that for young companies it provided an option that did not have such strict vetting requirements or regulations as the Listed Exchange, the USM or the Third Market. The principal disadvantage of the OTC was felt to be the lack of liquidity. Firms felt that their shares had poor marketability. Some firms identified an absence of regulation as a disadvantage of the OTC.

The survey revealed that for most firms using the OTC it was far from the preferred option. For 21% of respondents the OTC had been their only market at the time the sale of shares had become necessary or desirable. In most cases this meant that the distribution predated the USM and the Third Market and the firm did not qualify for Full Listing. Only 32% of respondents were able to identify any advantages to the market over the Stock Exchange, and 96% or 24 out of 25 respondents indicated a desire to seek Stock Exchange status in due course. Generally, the OTC was perceived, even by the firms within it, as no more than a stepping stone to one of the lower tier Stock Exchange markets.

20

Business Expansion Scheme funds

It was previously noted that the Government has been a leader in attempting to create an entrepreneurial, pro-business and pro-investment culture in the United Kingdom. One of the most concrete steps undertaken in this regard has been the establishment of the Business Expansion Scheme (BES). While it may be too early to judge its success as an investment vehicle, the first five years of the Business Expansion Scheme certainly appear to have raised the profile of unlisted equity investment among investors. More important, the BES would also appear to have raised the profile of venture capital investment as a source of finance among private companies and entrepreneurs. In 1988, BES funds accounted for 4% of all of the investments made by the member firms of the British Venture Capital Association.

Origins of the BES
The Business Expansion Scheme began life in 1981 as the Business Start-up Scheme (BSS), a programme whereby individual taxpayers in high margin tax bands could shelter some of their income from taxation through investing in shares of emerging (less than five years old) companies. The intention of the BSS was to flow investment from the skilled and successful wealthy into the hands of the emerging entrepreneurs. The intent was to channel skills as well as money, thus enhancing the likelihood of small business success. In practice however the BSS fell short of its goal. The original legislation was complex. The restrictions surrounding it, which were intended to prevent the BSS from becoming a mere tax dodge, made the Scheme largely unworkable. In 1981 the BSS managed to put £10 million into the hands of ten Business

Start-up Funds which pooled the resources of many investors, all of whom enjoyed the tax relief, and then invested in a portfolio of small companies. In 1982 the funds raised amounted to a mere £4 million.

In 1983 the BSS legislation was revised and the program renamed to its present styling. The BES removed some of the restrictions imposed by its predecessor, notably the restriction that investee companies need be new. The BES also removed the previously existing restriction that tax relief could apply only up to 50% of the cost of ordinary shares acquired. In 1986 the Scheme was further amended such that any shares issued after March 1986 would be exempt from capital gains tax. Finally, in that same budget of 1986 the Scheme was extended indefinitely.

The budget of 1988 placed a limit on the amount that any company could raise in one year, £500,000. Exceptionally, residential property companies can raise a total of £5,000,000.

As now constituted, rules and restrictions for investment under the BES are as follows:

1. Investors must be private individuals, not banks or other institutions.

2. BES investments are restricted to a maximum of £40,000 per annum (£80,000 in the case of couples). The minimum investment is £500.

3. Tax relief is granted only if and when contributions to a BES fund are invested in a recipient company.

4. Funds must be invested prior to the end of the fiscal year in order to qualify for tax relief.

5. Shares in investee companies must be held for five years.

6. A claw-back of tax relief will occur if the investee company goes public within three years.

7. Investors cannot invest in their own company under BES rules.

8. No investor may acquire more than 30% of an investee company.

9. Companies traded on a recognised exchange do not qualify for BES investment (the OTC excepted).

10. A limit of £500,000 may be raised in any year.

11. Capital gains derived from the sale of investments held for the full five years are exempt from tax.

12. Ordinary shares only may be issued under the BES.

When the legislation covering the BSS and BES was introduced, the Government allowed the formation of *Approved Investment Funds* which are to 'act as intermediaries for individuals wishing to have a spread of investments in a number of unquoted companies'. BES fund managers must be licensed securities dealers approved by Inland Revenue and the Department of Trade and Industry.

BES: aggregate investment

In 1988 78 BES related investments were made, representing 4% of the 1899 investments made by the members of the British Venture Capital Association at large. This means a decline from 1987 when 115 investments represented 6.7%.

All BES funds (BVCA members and non-members alike) supported 171 firms in 1986. BES investee firms represented a declining share of the total number of companies backed by the UK venture capital industry, down to 32.4% from 40.9% in 1984.

The average size of a BES investment has remained very stable during the past several years varying only marginally around an average of £168,000. By contrast, the average investment size for the UK venture capital industry as a whole, (as represented by the member firms of the BVCA) has increased from £273,000 to £546,000 since 1984.

BES: investment by sector and size

Consistent with the industry at large, BES related investments are swinging away from high technology and toward consumer related

	1983/84	1984/85	1985/86	1983–86
Number of Investments	242	297	219	758
Number of Companies	196	206	171	532
Volume Invested (£m)	41.2	49.6	36.4	127.3
Avg. Investment (£000)	170	167	166	168

Table 5.10　*Business Expansion Scheme – aggregate investment – 1983 to 1986*
Note: The BES investment year co-incides with the end of the fiscal year in April.
(Figures from Venture Economics)

companies. The former saw their relative share of funds increase from 32 to 55% between fiscal years 1984 and 1986, while the latter experienced a decline from 26% to under 10% during that same period. As with the industry at large, while medical/health and technology companies appear to be losing their appeal, these sectors continue to receive larger average investments than the consumer products sector. (Refer to Table 5.11.)

This trend reflects that professional investors are increasingly wary of sectors which have shown themselves to be especially volatile or cyclical.

BES investment tends to differ from other forms of venture capital finance in that it involves smaller amounts. It is notable that 116 separate investments, being two-thirds of the total number of investments made during fiscal 1986 involved less than £200,000. Less than 9% of all BES investment involved more than £500,000, a figure which is increasingly becoming the minimum cut-off for larger institutionally backed funds. (Refer to Table 5.12.) The reluctance of most non-BES venture capital funds to invest in these smaller propositions may not relate to fundamental risk, rather to the diseconomies of analysing and investing into business opportunities which would have little impact on their larger balance sheets.

BES: weaknesses and deficiencies

While the BES has surely proved a boon to investment in small and emerging companies in the UK, the scheme is not without its flaws and

| | % of Amount Invested | | | Total |
Industry Sector	1983/84	1984/85	1985/86	(£)
Consumer Related	32.3	34.2	55.5	50.5
Technology	25.9	16.0	9.2	22.0
Industrial/Manufg.	10.2	15.5	15.6	17.6
Medical/Health	5.6	7.1	2.2	6.6
Construction	7.9	4.6	1.4	6.1
Other Services	8.7	8.6	8.1	10.8
Other	9.4	14.0	8.0	13.7
TOTAL	100.0	100.0	100.0	127.3

Table 5.11 *Business Expansion Scheme – investment by industry sector – 1983 to 1986 (Figures from Venture Economics)*

Investment Size (£000)	Number of Financings	% of Financings	Amount (£m)	% of Amount
0–24	2	1.2	<0.1	<0.1
25–49	22	12.7	0.8	2.1
50–99	31	17.9	2.2	6.0
100–199	61	35.3	8.5	23.3
200–499	42	24.3	12.8	35.4
500–999	12	6.9	7.5	20.6
1000+	3	1.7	4.5	12.4
TOTAL	173	100	36.4	100

Table 5.12 *BES investment by size range in 1985/86*
Note: Authorised Investment Funds only
(*Figures from Venture Economics*)

deficiencies from the point of view of both the investor and the investee company.

The major criticism levied against the BES is the requirement that, in order to qualify for tax relief, investments need to be made before the end of the fiscal year. This restriction has the obvious effect of putting fund managers under a certain amount of pressure to 'perform', i.e. find suitable investments prior to the end of the fiscal year. This shifts the emphasis of investment away from the intention of the BES to find worthwhile investments, and toward the purely tax related aspect of the scheme.

Recent budgets have taken some steps to address the obvious problems caused by the time window aspect of BES investment. Beginning with fiscal year 1988, investments made in the first half of each fiscal year (i.e. during the period April to October) were eligible for tax relief retroactive to the prior year. However, the limit for such after the end of the tax year investments is just £5,000 per investor versus an overall limit of £40,000 investible into BES funds. While this measure may have helped to offset the seasonality of BES funding and investment, it was only a partial measure.

BES investments run the risk of violating one of the key rules of tax related investment: that the investment be sound in the first place, and that the tax relief be viewed only as a bonus. The time window aspect of BES investment may well increase the likelihood of investing under pressure in weak recipient companies. Fund performance may suffer as a result, thus making it more difficult for the fund manager to raise funds at some future date.

Another major criticism of the BES scheme is the restriction on investee companies' ability to gain full or USM listing. Gaining public listing is the venture capitalist's ultimate payoff, the 'exit' which the initial equity injection anticipated at origin. In a normal development capital environment, a public listing would be the culmination of a job well done. Under existing BES rules, an entrepreneur would hesitate to choose BES funding if he thought that the shareholders would be averse to going public at some time in the future.

BES backed businesses are barred from expanding into overseas markets, both manufacturing and export sales. Here again, the prohibition is on an activity which, in the normal course, would be the sign of a healthy, successful company.

The restriction against investing in one's own company may discourage hands-on entrepreneurship. For purposes of the Scheme, those deemed ineligible for tax relief are individuals who are controlling shareholders, their immediate families, substantial (over 30%) shareholders, employees or paid directors of the investee company. The result is that those who have the greatest stake in seeing a venture survive must invest after-tax income. Those who are more likely to be indifferent to the investee company's day-to-day operations provided their fiscal objectives are satisfied, are capable of investing pre-tax income.

BES financing may not suit the entrepreneur who seeks a relatively high level of funding but is not anxious to have a large number of partner/investors five years down the road. The £40,000 per investor limit on BES funding necessitates that larger investments be made through the pooled funds of a great many individuals. The entrepreneur seeking the maximum of £500,000 in a non-property company will find no less than 13 shareholders materialising once the fund has transferred ownership of the shares.

Finally, achieving liquidity may well prove a problem. The average BES fund investment, at £168,000, is about one half the size of the average investment for the venture capital industry as a whole. So too, many of the investee companies are too small for a public flotation.

The extent to which UK taxpayers will continue to contribute to BES funds will greatly depend on whether existing BES investments can be profitably realised. If investors discover that, after five years of holding

BES related shares, they are saddled with an illiquid investment in a still high-risk venture they will no doubt question in hindsight their early desire for tax relief at the expense of sound investment.

If, on the other hand, the first round of BES investments is successfully and profitably liquidated, either through an initial placement offering through the USM or by some other vehicle, then the BES will no doubt be judged a success. At present there remains significant scope for the scheme to grow.

The BES appears to have been particularly successful in encouraging small investments. At the end of fiscal year 1986 some 64% of BES investments (representing 10% by value) had been in amounts less than £100,000. The 1986 Survey of Business Expansion Scheme by Peat Marwick McLintock concluded:

> That 94% of finance invested by individuals would NOT have otherwise gone to particular companies.
>
> That 93% would NOT have been invested in UK unquoted companies.
>
> That 73% would NOT have been invested in equities in general.

Tony Lorenz cites in *Venture Capital Today* five examples of the means by which BES backed funds and independent or institutional backed venture capital companies can complement each other:

- The two may combine in instances where the entrepreneur may not want a single large investor, be it a BES fund or a venture capitalist.

- Where the financing may call for more than ordinary shares, since BES funds are restricted from buying preference or ordinary convertible shares. Non-BES funds can, of course, supply both of those things in addition to ordinary shares and debt.

- Where BES funds invest all of their available funds within the tax year, are unable to raise further funds but still have a deal flow from investee companies they wish to satisfy. Keeping in mind the next year's activities, they will give and seek friendly referrals.

- Where a BES fund has a proposition that exceeds its own limits for any single individual investment (say 20% of the total fund), in which case it will seek to syndicate the investment.

- Where a BES fund, having already invested in an attractive company, is unable to provide second stage financing because it has fully invested its existing pool of funds and cannot raise another.

The Business Expansion Scheme has served to raise the profile of unlisted equity investing both among investors and – more important – among investees. By providing a high profile, fiscally attractive means of investment in small and growth companies, the BES has stimulated the growth of venture capital investing in general.

21

The current environment and market opportunity: summary

The purpose of Part five was two fold:

- identify those elements which have contributed to the recent and dramatic growth of the venture capital investment industry in the UK;

- identify factors which suggest continuing market opportunities in this growing industry.

The text identified five broad areas, which on balance have had a positive and stimulating effect on the environment for venture capital investment in the United Kingdom. The areas identified were:

- fundamental changes in the structure of the economy;

- changes in the social and political environment;

- changes in the fiscal environment;

- changes in the economic environment;

- changes in the investment environment

The principal conclusions to be drawn are:

- The decline in traditional, smokestack, manufacturing industries has brought about a change in the types of business activity taking place in the UK. Traditional industries are being replaced by less capital intense, more service oriented firms.

- Employment growth is coming from the small firm sector. Large firms are actually shedding jobs.

- The number of new company registrations has increased dramatically since 1970.

- Financial institutions will have to seek their own growth through the financing of this expanding small and medium-sized firm sector.

There is a growing enterprise culture in the United Kingdom. While much of this cultural change may be attitudinal, there have been concrete examples where government policies have created a sympathetic environment for venture capital investing. It was noted that The Bank of England is a leading shareholder, and was a catalyst to the creation, of Investors in Industry (3i) as well as Equity Capital for Industry (ECI).

Through the Treasury, the government has also assisted in creating a sympathetic fiscal environment. Various fiscal measures which have benefited the UK's small firm sector were introduced. Specifically, reference was made to:

- tax breaks associated with venture capital investing by way of the Business Expansion Scheme;

- the reduction in small firm corporation tax rates;

- the steady, and continuing reduction of personal tax rates;

- the passage of certain amendments to the Companies Act, facilitating the repurchase of company shares.

During the past decade, a steady improvement in the economic environment has occurred. There have been significant changes in the investment environment. The creation of the Unlisted Securities Market, the Third Market, and the Over-the-Counter Market have all heightened awareness of equity finance in the small and medium sized firm sector, and have provided media for divestment which has added liquidity to the venture capital investment market. The Third Market and the Over-the-Counter Market both permit the selling of equity over a wider market without the loss of BES tax status (a boon to BES investing).

Finally, there is the Business Expansion Scheme itself. While the BES is responsible for a decreasing proportion of the total venture capital investment volume, this is in the context of an industry experiencing remarkable growth. The BES has proved a valuable stimulus to hundreds of emerging firms, and been an important element in the growing profile of venture capital finance.

Suppliers of venture capital in the United Kingdom

22

Suppliers of venture capital in the United Kingdom: introduction

It is important, in considering venture capital investment in the UK, that the reader has a knowledge of the existing suppliers of venture capital. In 1989 there are approximately 150 firms in the UK which claim to offer the venture capital product. These range from large publicly traded companies with a nationwide coverage of offices and an international reputation, to small, highly specialised and purely local concerns.

In the ensuing chapters, an examination will be made of the supply side of the UK venture capital market. The types of venture capital firm are discussed, and there follows an analysis of the characteristics of the venture capital investment firms of the UK.

Structure of Part six

Part six consists of two chapters. First, the various types of venture capital firms are defined. Five varieties of venture capital firm are identified, distinguished by their ownership. These are:

- bank captive funds;

- investment institution captive funds;

- independent private sector funds;

- Business Expansion Scheme funds;

- government backed or sponsored funds.

Second, a statistical profile is taken of the venture capital firms in the

United Kingdom. An analysis is made of:

- The number of venture capital firms.

- Their size:
    by pool of investible funds;
    by number of portfolio companies;
    by number of investment executives;
    by number of investments managed per executive.

- Their investment criteria:
    by minimum and maximum desired investment;
    by average investment size.

Finally, there is a brief summary and conclusion.

23

Types of venture capital firms

We saw in the introduction that UK venture capital firms are usually placed into five broad groupings distinguished by their ownership and/or their source of funds. Each of these groupings is discussed below.

Bank captive funds

It was during the mid-1970s, that the commercial banks began to experience a period of intense competition which manifested itself in two principal ways. The first was the decline in lending margins and the profitability of traditional lending business. The second was a move to extend and diversify the range of products and services available to bank customers. One sphere of activity which the banks entered in a tentative fashion was the provision of equity, as opposed to debt, capital.

A distinction is made between merchant bank and clearing bank captive venture funds. Merchant banks have long and integrally been involved in the equity investment business, whether as underwriters or as managers of listed equity portfolios. Clearing bank captive funds (those which are wholly owned by high street clearers) on the other hand, tend to function as distinct subsidiaries somewhat apart from the parent institution's primary activity: the provision of debt finance, at margin, generally for short maturity.

Clearing bank captive funds

Although all of the UK's high street clearing banks have a direct presence in the venture equity market, this presence continues to be small relative both to the size of the industry, and in relation to the overall size of the clearing banks themselves.

The UK's principal bank captive venture firms, their parent bank, and the year of start-up are listed below.

London Clearing Bank Subsidiaries	Parent Bank	Est'd.
Midland Montagu Ventures Limited	Midland Bank	1968
County NatWest Ventures Limited	National Westminster Bank	1972
Barclays Development Capital Ltd	Barclays Bank	1979
Lloyds Development Capital Limited	Lloyds Bank	1981
Hill Samuel Development Capital	TSB Bank	1982
Scottish Clearing Bank Subsidiaries		
Clydesdale Bank Equity Ltd	Clydesdale Bank	1981
The British Linen Bank Limited	Bank of Scotland	1972
Charterhouse Development Capital Ltd	Royal Bank of Scotland	1935
Other Bank Subsidiaries		
Citicorp Venture Capital Ltd	Citicorp	1980
AIIB Venture Capital	Allied Irish Banks	1971
Security Pacific Ventures Capital	Security Pacific Bank	1987
Scimitar Development Capital Limited	Standard Chartered Bank	1987

All of the above mentioned are wholly owned subsidiaries of their parent bank. Clearing and foreign bank venture capital subsidiaries exist for a number of reasons. One major consideration in establishing or acquiring a venture capital arm is the obvious profit potential brought to a bank's portfolio by devoting a share of its assets to long term financing. A second reason is the ability of a venture capital arm to inject equity to complement any debt financing that the lending arm of a bank might do. The maintenance of gearing ratios within acceptable limits might well make a previously 'unbankable' deal acceptable.

Unlike BES funds and the majority of independent venture capital funds, bank-backed venture capital companies tend to be open ended. That is to say that the amount of investment capital available to them is not predetermined, and is limited only by the parent bank's appetite for equity related financing deals. To date however (despite their sometimes

Bank Affiliated Venture Arm	Consolidated Group Capital (£m)	Venture Capital Pool (£m)	Venture as % of Capital
County NatWest Ventures	10,907	105	0.96
Barclays Development Capital	10,505	65	0.62
Lloyds Development Capital	5,867	40	0.68
Midland Montagu Ventures	5,499	150	2.72
Charterhouse Development Capital	2,152	242	11.25
British Linen Bank Fund Managers	1,446	37	2.56
Clydesdale Bank Equity	162	3	3.09

Table 6.1 *Investment in venture capital activities – clearing banks – Fye 1988*

high profile) bank captive venture capital funds represent only a small part of a banking group's total capital. The funds invested or available to the venture capital arms of the Big Four and the Scottish Clearers show a range between 0.55% and 7.83% of consolidated group capital. The average (mean) investment in venture capital activities was 3.10%. (Refer to Table 6.1.)

Investment institution captive funds

Investment institution captive funds are those which are wholly owned by fund managers, life assurance or pension companies. Examples of an institutional captive fund is Guinness Mahon Development Capital, or Hambro European Ventures, a wholly owned subsidiary of a prominent City institution.

Pension funds and insurance companies, already by far the largest players in the market for listed securities, hold a similar dominant position in the world of development capital. Of the approximately £1 billion of investible funds raised for venture capital investment over the past six years, approximately 40% has come from this sector.

Insurance firms

Historically, insurance firms have preferred to invest at arm's length, indirectly through independently managed venture capital companies. A recent development has been the growth of captive and semi-captive funds. These are venture capital firms funded by one or more financial institutions, one of which provides the investment management team. Examples of captive investment funds are CIN Industrial Investments Ltd, British Rail Pension Fund, and Norwich Union Venture Capital.

In 1980, Britain's largest insurance group, the Prudential Assurance Co established a £20m high technology fund named Prutec Ltd. Prutec specialises in start-up and early stage financing, and funds both companies and projects on an equal basis. With funds under management now exceeding £50m, Prutec has invested some £40m in more than 20 ventures since its founding.

Pension funds

CIN is a subsidiary of the National Coal Board Pension Funds, with responsibility for direct investment into start-up and development capital opportunities. Venture capital investments now account for some 15% of the National Coal Board Pension Fund's cash flow. Established in 1979, by 1985 CIN had invested some £170m. British Rail Pension Fund's strategy has been to provide development capital to established companies with proven products and/or management ability. Established in 1976, British Rail Pension Fund has invested more than £22m into development capital opportunities.

Independent funds

The independents are those corporate and other unaffiliated (i.e. with a bank or other institutional backer) funds whose ownership remains within the private sector. These funds have normally raised their capital from a variety of sources, although this category may include venture capital funds operated by subsidiaries of operating companies (so-called corporate venturing). Independent funds raise much of their capital from the institutional sector, typically from those firms not directly involved in venture capital investing through captive subsidiaries.

Business Expansion Scheme funds

Business Expansion Scheme funds are a special category of private sector venture funds. BES funds are funds created under the terms of the Business Expansion Scheme, a government created scheme whereby individuals can enjoy tax benefits from investing in privately owned, unlisted companies. BES funds may be managed by either investment institution captive fund managers or by independent private fund managers. An example of the BES fund manager is Hodgson Martin Ventures of Scotland.

Public sector funds

Public sector venture capital includes any equity capital fund wholly funded, either directly or indirectly by the Government. Principal among these the Scottish Development Agency, the Welsh Development Agency, the Highlands and Islands Development Board, the Northern Ireland Development Board and the British Technology Group.

Venture capital investment by type of investor

During the past four years there has been a dramatic decline in the

Investor Type	Percentage of Total Investment by Value			
	1985	1986	1987	1988
Captive Fund				
Clearing or Merchant Bank	26	24	16	15
Pension, Assurance, other	22	20	10	5
Independent Funds				
Private	32	31	28	38
Publicly traded	8	18	15	11
3i	n/a	n/a	26	28
BES Fund	10	6	4	2
Government	2	2	1	1

Table 6.2 *Venture capital investments by type of investor distribution by total value of investment UK – 1985 to 1988*
(Figures from Venture Economics)

importance of public sector venture capital. This decline is manifested in the falling market share of both direct vehicles, such as the Scottish and Welsh Development Agencies, and indirect vehicles, tax subsidised investments through the Business Expansion Scheme. (Refer to Table 6.2.)

24

The venture capital companies of the United Kingdom

As at year end 1988 there were approximately 150 firms, of varying sizes and investment orientations, providing venture and development capital in the United Kingdom. This list of players exceeds by one third the 113 venture capital firms reported at year end 1985. More remarkably, this number reflects a three and a half times increase in the size of the industry in just six years. (At the end of 1981 there were 41 such companies.)

It is envisaged that the growing number of players in the market will lead to greater degree of specialisation among individual players. These specialisations will probably be determined by one or more of the following variables:

- size of individual investments;
- stage of development of portfolio companies;
- technological intensity of portfolio companies;
- geographic location of portfolio companies;
- industry sector of portfolio companies.

Pool of investible funds

Twenty-eight venture capital firms belonging to the BVCA report a pool of investible capital of £10 million or less. Excluding 3i, whose open ended venture capital portfolio now exceeds £4 billion, the average UK investment pool at year end 1987 was £41 million. The larger funds

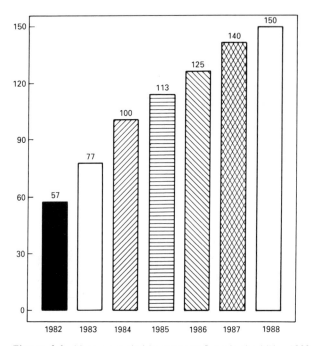

Figure 6.1 Venture capital investment firms in the UK – 1982–88

Pool of Investible Capital		Number of Firms	% of Survey
less than	£ 5,000,000	12	11.1
£ 5,000,001 to	£ 10,000,000	17	15.7
£10,000,001 to	£ 25,000,000	21	19.4
£25,000,001 to	£ 50,000,000	12	11.1
£50,000,001 to	£100,000,000	22	20.4
more than	£100,000,000	24	22.2
total sample size		= 108	100.0

Table 6.3 *Size of BVCA members – pool of investible funds – 1988*
(*Figures from BVCA*)
Note: Many venture funds are open ended, i.e. have unlimited or unspecified capital at their disposal. The majority of bank-captive venture funds are open ended. Where a fund has no specified limit, the volume of funds already invested is indicated.

include the London-based bank affiliates (Charterhouse Development Capital – £180 million invested), the American banks (Citicorp Development Capital – £80 million invested) and the major pension funds and insurance companies (Prudential Venture Managers – £150 million invested). (Refer to Table 6.3.)

The size of a venture capital firm's investment pool will, to a large extent, depend on the proportion of the portfolio that the firm intends to devote to later stage financings (particularly management buy-outs) with their greater capital requirements. The importance of the figures given in Table 6.3 is that they suggest that size, in terms of capital invested, need not be a barrier to entry for new suppliers seeking to move into the venture capital industry.

Investments

Investment executives

Fully one third of all BVCA members employ up to four full time investment executives. More than two-thirds of the member firms employ up to eight. Excluding 3i, with a staff of 750 venture capital executives (substantially the largest venture capital firm in the world), the average firm employs slightly more than nine professional investing staff. It would appear that a large staff is not a prerequisite for entering into the venture capital field.

Investments per executive

At the end of 1988, one third of the UK's venture capital firms indicated that their venture capital executives managed fewer than four investments each. (Refer to Table 6.4.) The average venture capital executive manages a portfolio of between six and seven investments.

This average may reflect the large number of young venture capital firms which are fully staffed but not yet fully invested. As these companies continue to find investment opportunities, and the pool of funds becomes invested, one can expect to see the average number of companies managed by one individual rise.

Given the time intensive nature of the 'due diligence' process, and the labour intensive nature of certain hands-on investments, one would expect a limited number of companies per investment officer.

Investments/executive	Firms	% of Sample
0 – 2	11	10%
>2 – 4	25	23%
>4 – 6	20	19%
>6 – 8	19	18%
>8 –10	13	12%
> 10–15	9	8%
> 15	11	10%
Total	108	100%

Table 6.4   *Number of investments per executive*
(Figures from the BVCA)

Number of investments

Despite the advantages of portfolio diversification, a large proportion of UK venture capital firms (37%) have investments in fewer than 25 firms.

The median portfolio size was 40 investments, little changed from the 39 investments in the median portfolio in 1987. The range was from 0 investments to the 5000 venture capital investments reported by 3i.

Excluding 3i's portfolio (whose 5,000 investments accounted for nearly 50% of the 10,140 total), the average venture capital portfolio

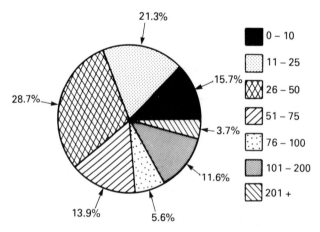

Figure 6.2   Number of Investments in venture capital portfolios – 1988. (Figures from the BVCA)

consisted of 54 investments, down from 60 in 1987. (Refer to Figure 6.2.)

The significance of these figures is the fact that many UK venture capital firms maintain investment portfolios which, in a relative sense, are small.

Investment size

The majority of UK venture capitalists in the UK indicate a willingness to invest relatively small amounts of money – given the right proposition.

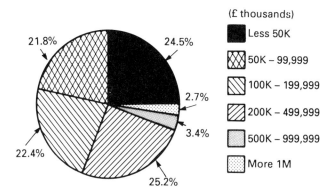

Figure 6.3 UK venture capital firms – minimum desired investment – 1987. (Figures from Peat Marwick McLintock)

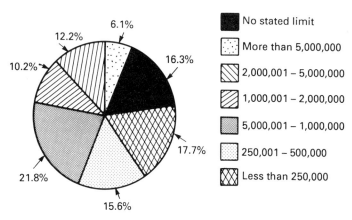

Figure 6.4 UK venture capitalist firms – maximum desired investment – 1987. (Figures from Peat Marwick McLintock)

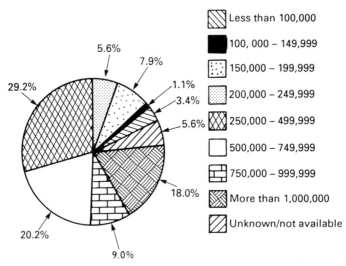

Figure 6.5 UK venture capitalist firms – average investment size – 1987

One quarter (24.5%) of all UK venture firms responding to the 1987 survey, *Major Sources of Venture Capital in the UK* by Peat Marwick McLintock advised that they were willing to invest less than £50,000. Slightly less than one half will consider investing involving less than £100,000. (Refer to Figure 6.3.)

A willingness to provide smaller amounts of capital, in the case of the 'right' proposition, does not appear to have helped bridge the so-called 'venture capital gap'. Generally, (in more than 80% of the cases), UK venture capital firms' average investment exceed £250,000. For more than a third, in fact, the average investment size exceeds £750,000. (Refer to Figure 6.5.)

In 1988, the average venture capital investment by the membership of the BVCA was £957,000. Nearly one fifth of all venture capital firms invested an average of more than £1,000,000.

Notwithstanding their enunciated willingness to provide smaller amounts of capital, in practise the majority of the UK's venture capital firms have fairly high investment floors.

25

Suppliers of venture capital in the United Kingdom: summary

In the preceding chapters, we looked into the supply side of the UK venture capital market. The types of venture capital firm were noted, followed by a statistical analysis of the characteristics of the venture capital investment firms of the United Kingdom. The findings of this chapter are as follows:

Five varieties of venture capital firm can be identified, distinguished by their ownership. These are:

- bank captive funds;

- investment institution captive funds;

- independent private sector funds;

- Business Expansion Scheme funds;

- government backed or sponsored funds.

During the past five years there has been a steady decline in the share of total investment supplied by the public sector. The overall rapid growth in the industry suggests that this decline is relative rather than absolute, and that early public sector leadership in the arena of venture capital investing has led to a significant growth in private sector venture capital activity.

The number of venture capital firms in the UK is growing rapidly. It is envisioned that this growth will lead to an increasing need for venture capital suppliers to (a) segment the market and (b) differentiate themselves, perhaps through specialisation.

One third of all UK venture capital investment firms have a capital pool of less than £10,000,000. It is concluded that scale, in terms of pool of funds, is not a significant barrier to entry.

One third of all UK venture capital investment firms have a portfolio of 25 investee companies or fewer. The median portfolio size lies between 26 and 50 investments. While recognising the importance of portfolio diversification, it is again concluded that size need not be an initial barrier to entry.

One third of all UK venture capital investment firms employ four or fewer full time venture capital investment executives. Two thirds employ eight or fewer. It is concluded that staff size need not be a barrier to entry.

The average venture capital investment executive manages less than seven portfolio investments. This average may reflect the fact that many venture capital firms are still young and not yet fully invested. However, the small number of investments per executive would also appear to confirm the labour intensive nature of venture capital portfolio management.

Nearly one half of all UK venture capital firms claim to be willing to invest less than £100,000 in any individual proposition. In 1988, however, the UK's actual average investment size was £957,000. Of the 87 venture capital investment firms reporting to a 1987 survey, only 11 (12.4%) reported investing an average of less than £200,000. It is concluded that, despite an enunciated willingness to provide smaller amount of capital, in practice the majority of UK venture capital firms have fairly high investment floors.

Glossary

arm's length investment. An investment in which the investor exercises no day-to-day influence or control over the investee company.

basis point. One hundredth of one per cent (0.01%).

bear market. An investment climate characterised by rising share prices or the expectation of rising share prices.

BES. The Business Expansion Scheme. A public sector scheme to promote tax-efficient venture capital investments by the private sector.

book value. An accounting term meaning the value of a company as calculated by subtracting its total liabilities from its total assets.

BTG. The British Technology Group. A public sector venture capital company and one of the prime practitioners of high technology investment in the UK.

bull market. An investment climate characterised by falling share prices or the expectation of falling share prices.

business plan. A formal written proposal for obtaining finance. The business plan will include a complete, but succinct, description of the business, its management and operations, and its current and planned state of affairs. The business plan will typically be a venture capital company's first exposure to a potential investee business.

BVCA. The British Venture Capital Association. The principal industry association and lobby group for venture capital firms in the UK.

capital. The ownership interest in a business; assets or resources.

capital gain. The profit obtained when an investor sells an asset for more than the original purchase value.

Chinese wall. An insurmountable barrier. Usually used in the context of the separation of two sides of a business. The barrier to prevent a conflict of interest or the appearance of a conflict of interest.

common share. Also known as ordinary share. It represents an ownership stake in a company. It is characterised by the ability of the share holder to share in the profits of the venture.

creditor. One to whom a sum of money is owed.

deal flow. The flow of business plans or venture capital proposals which form the life blood of a venture capitalist's activity.

debt. A sum of money that is owed; an obligation to pay or perform.

development capital. The finance provided to fund the expansion or growth of a company which is breaking even or trading at a small profit.

due diligence. The process of performing detailed verification of an investee company's financial and management information prior to making an investment.

early stage finance. Finance provided to companies that have completed the product development stage and required further funds to initiate commercial manufacturing and sales. They will not yet be generating profit.

earn out. The realisation of a venture capital investment through entrepreneur's acquisition of the shares with the proceeds of his own earnings flow.

entrepreneur. The owner or manager of a business enterprise who, by risk and initiative, attempts to make profits.

equity. The interest of ordinary shareholders in a company; an ownership right or share.

equity gap. The term applied to the perception that UK venture capital investors are unwilling to provide equity finance below a certain minimum investment.

EVCA. The European Venture Capital Association. The principal industry association and lobby group for venture capital firms located in Western Europe.

executive director. A member of a company's Board of Directors who also serves in a full-time executive capacity as an employee of the company.

exit. The realisation of a venture capital investment, normally by flotation, trade-sale or an earn-out.

expansion capital. *See* DEVELOPMENT CAPITAL.

flotation. Often the desired form of exit for a venture capital investment; the selling of an investee companies' shares on a publicly traded stock market.

follow-on finance. *See* SECOND ROUND FINANCE.

gearing. *See* LEVERAGE.

hands-off. The arm's length or non-involvement of a venture capitalist in the management of an investee company.

hands-on. The active involvement of a venture capital investor, at the Board level, in the overall strategic direction and management of an investee company.

hurdle rate. The minimum required rate of return on a capital investment.

illiquid. A term to describe an investment which cannot readily be converted to cash.

income. The flow of dividends (whether from common or preferred shares) realised on a venture capital investment.

investee. A venture or entrepreneurial firm into which a venture capitalist has invested money.

IPO. Initial Placement Offering. An offer to sell a company's shares on a public stock exchange for the first time.

IPR. Intellectual Property Rights. A claim on intellectual, as opposed to tangible property, normally in the form of patents, licences or copyrights.

IRR. Internal Rate of Return. The rate at which an investment's cash flows discount to £0.

LBO. Leveraged Buy Out. A buy-out involving a high degree of leverage, or gearing, with debt supplementing the entrepreneur's and the venture capitalist's equity.

leverage. The ratio of a company's debt of equity capital. The ability of a firm to incur debt against its equity.

liquid investment. An investment which can readily be converted to cash.

liquidity. The measure of a venture capitalist's ability to convert its investment to cash.

listed company. A company whose shares are traded on the main market of the Stock Exchange.

maturity. The date upon which an investment becomes recouped. Of a loan, the repayment date; of a venture capital investment, realisation through the sale of shares.

MBI. Management Buy In. Funds provided to enable a manager or group of managers from outside the company to buy-in to the company with the support of venture capital investors.

MBO. Management Buy Out. Funds provided to enable current management and investors to acquire an existing product line or business.

mezzanine finance. The stage of financing supplied to a private company in the final run up to a trade sale or a public flotation.

multiple. The ratio of a company's share price to its earnings per share.

non-executive director. A member of a company's Board of Directors who does not hold an executive position nor full-time employment with the firm.

ordinary shares. *See* COMMON SHARES.

OTC. Over the counter. The over-the-counter market is a stock market which trades in the shares of companies not recognised by the Stock Exchange.

portfolio. The complete range of investments held by an individual investor or a financial organisation.

preference share. A share normally characterised by a lack of voting rights which in return confers a contractural dividend pay out.

quoted company. A company whose shares are traded on a public stock exchange.

realisation. The process of bringing to fruition or make concrete a venture capital investment to sell or make into cash one's stake in a business.

ROE. Return On Equity. The yield or return on an investor's equity or share capital investment. ROE is normally stated as a percentage per annum.

ROI. Return On Investment. The overall yield or return on an investor's investment. ROI is normally stated as percentage per annum.

SDA. The Scottish Development Agency. A major public sector venture capital company located in Scotland.

second round finance. The provision of capital to a firm which has previously been in receipt of external capital but whose financial needs have subsequently expaneled.

security. A financial asset represented by a claim or a certificate, such as a bond, a promissory note or a share certificate.

seed capital. The financing of the initial product development or a capital provided to an entrepreneur to prove the feasibility of a project and qualify for start-up capital.

start-up capital. Capital needed to finance the product development, initial marketing and the establishment of product facilities.

syndicate. An association of venture capital firms organised to undertake an investment project requiring a large sum of capital.

take out. The realisation of a venture capital investment through the acquisition of one investor's shares by another.

Third Market. The most recently inaugurated, and lowest, tier of the Stock Exchange.

3i. The trade name for Investors In Industry plc, the world's largest venture capital investment organisation.

trade sale. The realisation of an investment through the sale of the company to a competitor or customer firm.

unquoted company. A company whose shares are not traded on a recognised Stock Exchange.

USM. The Unlisted Securities Market. The second tier of the Stock Exchange, established in 1980 in order to provide access to firms that were too young or too small to obtain a full listing.

valuation. Formal assessment of the worth of a venture for purposes of determining its flotation or disposal value.

venture. A commercial undertaking characterised by risk of loss as well as opportunity for profit.

Wilson Committee. *See Wilson Report.*

Wilson Report. Committee report on the functioning of financial institutions. Led by former Prime Minister Sir Harold Wilson, this government appointed committee undertook a wide-ranging examination of the UK's financial institutions and their effectiveness in flowing funds in the nation's businesses.

yield. The profit or return from an investment, usually expressed as a percentage of its cost or current value.

Bibliography

The Attitudes of Top US and UK Executives towards Venture Capital and its Applications, British Venture Capital Association, May 1986

Batchelor, C., 'Europe takes Lead in Venture Capital', *Financial Times*, 27 May 1988

Batchelor, C., 'Prospects Good for Cross-Border Investment', *Financial Times*, May 1988

Batchelor, C., '3i Team Set Up to Supply Know-How for "Buy-Ins"', *Financial Times*, 22 June 1988

Building Tomorrow" *Profitable Businesses – Viewpoints and Recommendations*, British Venture Capital Association, April 1986

Bruce, L., 'Venture Capital Seeks Pan-European Base', *International Management Journal*, April 1987

Burns, P. and Dewhurst, J., *Small Business in Europe*, Macmillan Education Ltd., London, 1986

Cary, L., 'Guide to Venture Capital in the UK', *The Venture Capital Report*, Pitman Publishing, 1985

Clark, R., *Venture Capital in Britain, America and Japan*, Croom Helm, London, 1987

Cohen, R., 'Venture Capital After the Crash of '87', *Info EVCA*, 2nd issue, 1988

Committee to Review the Functioning of Financial Insitutions, *Research Report No. 1 – Survey of Investment Attitudes and Financing of Medium-sized Companies*, HMSO, London, 1979

Dawkins, W., 'Small Businesses', *Financial Times*, 30 April 1985

Fates, R.J., 'Mezzanine Debt in Management Buy-Outs', *Acquisitions Monthly*, November 1986

Fells, G., 'Venture Capital in Canada – A Ten Year Review', *The Business Quarterly*, Spring 1984

Financing Tomorrow's Winners – Conference Papers, Financial Times Conference Organisation, October 1986

Foster, C.A.D., *The Third Market*, Unpublished Undergraduate Dissertation, University of Stirling, 1988

Hambros Company Guide, 1987

Hutchinson, H., 'Mezzanine Debt – a Flexible Form of Finance', *Acquisitions Monthly*, November 1987

Improving Venture Capital Opportunities in Europe – Proceedings of the Symposium on Improving Venture Capital Opportunities in Europe, Commissioner of the European Committees, Brussels, 1985

The Internationalisation of Venture Capital, European Venture Capital Association Conference Speakers' Papers, Financial Times Conference Organisation, May 1988

Kostuch, M.J., 'Venture Capital Financing Builds Successful Companies', *The Business Quarterly*, Spring 1974

Lloyd, S., 'UK Venture Capital – The Next Phase of Growth', *Venture Capital Report Limited*, 1988

Lorenz, T., *Venture Capital Today – A Guide to the Venture Capital Market in the United Kingdom*, Woodhead-Faulkner Ltd., Cambridge, 1985

Lowenstein, P., *Recent Development in Institutionally-Backed Pools of Capital for Financing Corporate Restructuring in Canada*, Presentation to the Financial Post Conference, 7 October 1986

Mason, C., 'Venture Capital in the United Kingdom, A Geographic Perspective', *National Westminster Bank Quarterly Review*, May 1987

The Operation and Effectiveness of the Business Expansion Scheme, Small Business Research Trust, May 1985

Owen, P., 'Insights into Raising Venture Capital' *Business Graduate Journal*, January 1987

Preece, D.C.E., *The Venture Capital industry in Northern Ireland* Unpublished dissertation, Stirling University, 1987

Raising Venture Capital – An Entrepreneur's Guidebook, Deloitte, Haskins and Sells, UK 1984

Report on Investment Activity 1985, British Venture Capital Association, 1986

Report on Investment Activity – 1986, British Venture Capital Association, 1987

Report on Investment Activity – 1987, British Venture Capital Association, 1988

Report on Investment Activity – 1988, British Venture Capital Association, 1989

Research Report No. 3 – Studies of Small Firms Financing, HMSO, London, 1979

Smith, S.J., *Is the Over-the-Counter Market a Viable Option?*, Unpublished dissertation, University of Stirling, 1988

Stoy Howard, *The Essence of USM Success*, London, 1988

Survey on the Impact of Venture Capital, Arthur Andersen & Co. and British Venture Capital Association, 1986

Tyzoon, Tyebjee, T., and Bruno, A.V., 'Venture Capital Decision Making: Preliminary Results from Three Empirical Studies', *Frontiers in Entrepreneurship Research*, Babson College, 1981

USM Survey, Peat Marwick McLintock, July 1987

'Venture Capital', survey in the *Financial Times*, 4 December 1987 and 8 December 1986

Venture Capital in Europe, Peat Marwick McLintock and the European Venture Capital Association, 1987, 1988, 1989

Venture Magazine, Vol. 9, No. 8, January 1986

Webb, I., *Management Buy-out – A Guide for the Prospective Entrepreneur*, Gower Publishing Company Ltd., 1985

Wilmot, T., *Inside the Over-the-Counter Market*, Woodhead-Faulkner, 1985

Wilson, J.W., *The New Venturers – Inside the High Stakes World of Venture Capital*, Addison-Wesley Publishing Company, Massachusetts, 1986

Appendix:
BVCA membership list

Company:	**ABACUS DEVELOPMENT CAPITAL LTD**
Address:	Dammas House, Dammas Lane, Swindon SN1 3EJ
Telephone:	0793 618130
Telex:	444866 DAMMAS G
Fax:	0793 618129

Company Details

Full-time Executives:	5
Type of Organisation:	Independent
Funds Managed:	Abacan
	Several private unnamed funds
Total Capital Invested:	£7m
Total Capital Available:	£25m
Specialisations:	Manufacturing & industrial, food and drink
Current Portfolio Size:	18
Investments as Lead Investor:	

Investment Preferences

Minimum Investment:	£100,000
Preferred Investment:	£250,000 & £1m over 3 year period
Type of Funding:	Flexible but always with an equity stake
Stage of Investment:	All stages supported
Investment Conditions:	No preconceptions; back strong and receptive management teams
Industry Preferences:	General Industrial & Manufacturing, Food & Drink and property deals
Geographical Preferences:	UK

Contacts:	Philip Davenport, John Hall-Craggs, Thomas Kier, Wendy Pollecoff, Nicholas Reynolds

Company:	**ABERDEEN FUND MANAGERS LIMITED**
Address:	10 Queen's Terrace, Aberdeen AB9 1QJ
Telephone:	0224 631999
Telex:	73683 ABERFM G
Fax:	0224 647010

Company Details

Full-time Executives:	12
Type of Organisation:	Independent – Shares owned by Executive Managers and Ensign Trust PLC
Funds Managed:	North of Scotland Investment Company plc is the principal vehicle for unquoted investment. In addition the company manages the Abtrust range of Unit Trusts, North Of Scotland Finance Company Limited; Pension Funds; Private client portfolios.
Total Capital Invested:	£5m
Total Capital Available:	£5m
Specialisations:	None
Current Portfolio Size:	15
Investments as Lead Investor:	Not disclosed

Investment Preferences

Minimum Investment:	£50,000
Preferred Investment:	£200,000 to £500,000
Type of Funding:	Primarily equity
Stage of Investment:	Expansion, buy-out, development. Start ups only in exceptional circumstances
Investment Conditions:	No fixed criteria
Industry Preferences:	None
Geographical Preferences:	Scotland

Contact:	Andrew A. Laing

Company:	**ABINGWORTH plc**
Address:	26 St. James's Street, London SW1A 1HA
Telephone:	01–839 6745

Telex:	946066
Fax:	01–930 1891

Company Details

Full-time Executives:	6
Type of Organisation:	Independent
Funds Managed:	Abingworth plc
	Interven Capital SA
	Interven II SA
	Tetraven Fund SA
	Biotechnology Venture Fund SA
Total Capital Invested:	Abingworth £68m;
	Managed Funds: $70m
Total Capital Available:	Abingworth: As above
	Managed Funds: $38m
Specialisations:	USA; Biotechnology & Health Care
Current Portfolio Size:	83
Investments as	
Lead Investor:	Garfunkels PLC; The Melville Group Limited; Spice PLC; British Bio-technology Limited

Investment Preferences

Minimum Investment:	£250,000
Preferred Investment:	£500,000–£1m
Type of Funding:	Equity only
Stage of Investment:	All stages
Investment Conditions:	Management of proven ability
Industry Preferences:	New technology, high growth industries and sectors
Geographical Preferences:	USA, UK

Contacts:	Hon A.T.S. Montagu (Chairman), P.F. Dicks, D.W. Quysner, D.J. Morrison, D.F.J. Leathers, Dr S.W. Bunting

Company:	**ADVENT LTD**
Address:	25 Buckingham Gate, London SW1E 6LD
Telephone:	01–630 9811
Telex:	296923 ADVENT G
Fax:	01–828 4919

Company Details

Full-time Executives:	10

Type of Organisation:	Independent
Funds Managed:	Advent Technology
	Advent Eurofund
	Advent Capital
	Advent Euroventures
	Advent Performance Materials Limited Partnership
	Advent First Limited Partnership
Total Capital Invested:	£70m
Total Capital Available:	£50m
Specialisations:	High Technology
Current Portfolio Size:	67
Investments as	
Lead Investor:	European Silicon Structures SA; Computer Security International Ltd; National Telecommunications plc; Orthofix BV

Investment Preferences

Minimum Investment:	£300,000
Preferred Investment:	£1m +
Type of Funding:	Equity
Stage of Investment:	All stages
Investment Conditions:	No fixed criteria
Industry Preferences:	None, but specialists in high technology
Geographical Preferences:	Worldwide

Contact:	Colin Amies

Company:	**ADVENT MANAGEMENT OPPORTUNITIES LTD**
Address:	25 Buckingham Gate, London SW1E 6LD
Telephone:	01–630 9811
Telex:	—
Fax:	01–828 9958

Company Details

Full-time Executives:	5
Type of Organisation:	Independent
Funds Managed:	Advent First Limited Partnership
	Advent Management Opportunities LP
	Management Opportunities LP
Total Capital Invested:	£6m

Total Capital Available:	£40m
Specialisations:	Backing management into existing companies to build a substantial business
Current Portfolio Size:	4
Investments as Lead Investor:	Home Improvement Industries Ltd.; Pegasus Group plc

Investment Preferences

Minimum Investment:	£500,000
Preferred Investment:	£1m–£10m
Type of Funding:	Equity
Stage of Investment:	Expansion and management buy-in
Investment Conditions:	None
Industry Preferences:	None
Geographical Preferences:	UK and Europe

Contacts:	John Nash, Trevor Jenkins, Jessica Knight

Company:	**AIIB VENTURE CAPITAL**
Address:	Pinners Hall, 8/9 Austin Friars, London EC2N 2AE
Telephone:	01–920 9155
Telex:	8952354
Fax:	01–628 3319

Company Details

Full-time Executives:	14 (London based 4)
Type of Organisation:	Merchant Bank Venture Capital Group – Subsidiary of Allied Irish Banks plc
Funds Managed:	Allied Combined Trust Ltd
	Allied Irish Investment Company Ltd
	Allied Irish Venture Capital Ltd
	First Venture Fund Limited
Total Capital Invested:	£60m
Total Capital Available:	Open
Specialisations:	None
Current Portfolio Size:	45
Investments as Lead Investor:	Albright & Wilson Ireland Ltd; Heiton Holdings plc; Barlo Group plc; Etos Investments Ltd; Noble Industries plc

Investment Preferences

Minimum Investment:	£200,000
Preferred Investment:	£200,000–£1,500,000 (larger amounts syndicated)
Type of Funding:	Equity and Equity/Loan packages
Stage of Investment:	Expansion/Development Capital/Buy-outs, Start-up in specific circumstances
Investment Conditions:	None
Industry Preferences:	None
Geographical Preferences:	UK and Ireland

Contacts:	Brian Stephens, Philip Wilson, Michael Potts, Ian Hudson, Niall Carrol (Dublin)

Company:	**ALAN PATRICOF ASSOCIATES LIMITED (APA)**
Address:	24 Upper Brook Street, London W1Y 1PD
Telephone:	01–872 0015
Telex:	265451
Fax:	01–629 9035

Company Details

Full-time Executives:	9
Type of Organisation:	Independent
Funds Managed:	APA Venture Capital Fund
	APA Ventures II
	APA Ventures III
Total Capital Invested:	£56m
Total Capital Available:	£115m
Specialisations:	Biotechnology/Healthcare, Computers, Consumer goods & services, Media & Publishing, Retail, Telecommunications
Current Portfolio Size:	42 UK
Investments as Lead Investor:	Computacenter Limited; My Kinda Town Group Limited; National Telecommunications plc; Rotaprint Industries Limited; The Sterling Publishing Group plc

Investment Preferences

Minimum Investment:	None
Preferred Investment:	£500,000–£5m
Type of Funding:	Primarily equity
Stage of Investment:	Start-up, expansion, buy-out, later stage, rescue
Investment Conditions:	None
Industry Preferences:	None
Geographical Preferences:	None

Contacts: Ronald Cohen, Adrian Beecroft, Peter Englander, Cyril Freedman, Hamish Hale, Clive Sherling, Jeffrey Wilkinson

Company:	**ALTA BERKELEY ASSOCIATES**
Address:	9 Savile Row, London W1X 1AF
Telephone:	01–734 4884
Telex:	—
Fax:	01–734 6711

Company Details

Full-time Executives:	6
Type of Organisation:	Independent
Funds Managed:	Alta-Berkeley Limited Partnership
	Alta-Berkeley Eurofund L.P.
	Alta-Berkeley L.P.II
Total Capital Invested:	$35m
Total Capital Available:	£30m
Specialisations:	Healthcare/Life sciences, Electronics, Media and Information Services
Current Portfolio Size:	24
Investments as Lead Investor:	Analick Developments, Corin Medical Limited; Christiaens International; Precision Software, Protein Separations

Investment Preferences

Minimum Investment:	£100,000
Preferred Investment:	£500,000
Type of Funding:	Equity
Stage of Investment:	Start-up, Early Stage, Development, Buy-out
Investment Conditions:	None

Industry Preferences:	Healthcare/Life sciences, electronics, media and information services. Will consider new technologies in other high growth industry sectors
Geographical Preferences:	UK & Continental Europe

Contacts:	Bryan Wood, Laurie Rostron, David Needham, Massimo Prelz

Company:	**B & C VENTURES LIMITED**
Address:	King's House, 36–37 King Street, London EC2V 8BE
Telephone:	01–726 4070
Telex:	884095 BCHOLD
Fax:	01–600 0733

Company Details

Full-time Executives:	7
Type of Organisation:	Independent
Funds Managed:	Own funds
Total Capital Invested:	£35m
Total Capital Available:	£100m
Specialisations:	None
Current Portfolio Size:	30
Investments as Lead Investor:	Norwest Holst Holdings Limited; The Imtec Group PLC; Cifer PLC

Investment Preferences

Minimum Investment:	£500,000
Preferred Investment:	£1–£15m
Type of Funding:	Flexible
Stage of Investment:	All stages considered
Investment Conditions:	None
Industry Preferences:	None
Geographical Preferences:	None

Contacts:	Ian Hislop, Richard Wevill

Company:	**BAILLIE GIFFORD TECHNOLOGY LTD**
Address:	10 Glenfinlas Street, Edinburgh EH3 6YY
Telephone:	031–225 2581
Telex:	72310 BGCO G

Fax:	031–225 2358

Company Details

Full-time Executives:	3
Type of Organisation:	Independent
Funds Managed:	Baillie Gifford Technology plc
	The Scottish Mortgage and Trust plc
	The Monks Investment Trust plc
Total Capital Invested:	£15m
Total Capital Available:	£5m
Specialisations:	None
Current Portfolio Size:	24
Investments as	
Lead Investor:	Intelligent Applications Ltd; Intelligent Environments; Redwood International Ltd; Hybrid Memory Products Ltd

Investment Preferences

Minimum Investment:	£100,000
Preferred Investment:	£300,000
Type of Funding:	Equity
Stage of Investment:	Start-up, Expansion
Investment Conditions:	None
Industry Preferences:	High Technology and others
Geographical Preferences:	UK, USA, Europe

Contact:	John Marsden

Company:	**BARCLAYS DEVELOPMENT CAPITAL LIMITED**
Address:	Pickfords Wharf, Clink Street, London SE1 9DG
Telephone:	01–407 2389
Telex:	914912 BDCL G
Fax:	01–407 3362

Company Details

Full-time Executives:	12
Type of Organisation:	Clearing Bank Subsidiary
Funds Managed:	Own funds and adviser to BZW Buy-Out Trust
Total Capital Invested:	£64.9m
Total Capital Available:	Unlimited

Specialisations:	Various
Current Portfolio Size:	108 (gross), 76 (net after realisations)
Investments as	
Lead Investor:	Schreiber Furniture; Bath Plant Group Ltd; GD Underwood Ltd; NE Technology Ltd; Gold Crown Foods Ltd

Investment Preferences

Minimum Investment:	£150,000
Preferred Investment:	£500,000–£5.0m
Type of Funding:	Equity, Equity/Loan
Stage of Investment:	Some expansion but mainly buy-out
Investment Conditions:	—
Industry Preferences:	None
Geographical Preferences:	None

Contacts:	M.R. Cumming, L.A.C. Horler

Company:	**BARCLAYS VENTURE CAPITAL UNIT**
Address:	Clerkenwell House, 67 Clerkenwell Road, London EC1R 5BH
Telephone:	01–242 4900
Telex:	—
Fax:	01–242 2048

Company Details

Full-time Executives:	4
Type of Organisation:	Part of Barclays Bank plc
Funds Managed:	Barclays Baronsmead Fund (co-managed with Baronsmead Plc)
Total Capital Invested:	New fund
Total Capital Available:	An initial £20m
Specialisations:	None
Current Portfolio Size:	New fund
Investments as	
Lead Investor:	New fund

Investment Preferences

Minimum Investment:	£100,000
Preferred Investment:	£250,000 +
Type of Funding:	Equity (debt from Barclays Bank)

Stage of Investment:	All but emphasis on expansion/replacement
Investment Conditions:	Only available to Barclays customers – otherwise flexible
Industry Preferences:	None
Geographical Preferences:	Great Britain

Contacts:	Brian Worsfold or Michael Vallance

Company:	**BARING BROTHERS HAMBRECHT & QUIST LIMITED**
Address:	140 Park Lane, London W1Y 3AA
Telephone:	01–408 0555
Telex:	295082 BBHQ G
Fax:	01–493 5153

Company Details

Full-time Executives:	10
Type of Organisation:	Independent
Funds Managed:	Not disclosed
Total Capital Invested:	$40m (June 1988)
Total Capital Available:	$95m (June 1988)
Specialisations:	None
Current Portfolio Size:	56 (June 1988)
Investments as	
Lead Investor:	Data Integrity Holdings; Book Data; DH Group; European Educational Software; New Focus Healthcare

Investment Preferences

Minimum Investment:	No minimum
Preferred Investment:	Up to £1m
Type of Funding:	Equity
Stage of Investment:	All stages
Investment Conditions:	Prefer businesses or start-ups with international potential
Industry Preferences:	None
Geographical Preferences:	UK, Europe, USA, Japan

Contacts:	Richard Onians, Paul Bailey, Jeremy Brassington, Richard Furse

Company:	**BARING CAPITAL INVESTORS LTD**
Address:	140 Park Lane, London W1Y 3AA
Telephone:	01–408 1282
Telex:	295082
Fax:	01–493 1368

Company Details

Full-time Executives:	3 (in London), 2 (Paris), 2 (Munich)
Type of Organisation:	Indirect & wholly owned subsidiary of Barings plc
Funds Managed:	Baring European Capital Trust
	Baring European Capital FCPR
	Baring European Buy-Out Partnership LP
Total Capital Invested:	ECU 28m
Total Capital Available:	ECU 65m
Specialisations:	None
Current Portfolio Size:	10
Investments as	
Lead Investor:	Allevard (Fr); HPP (Fr); Kontron (It); Lignotock (Ger); Bricom (UK)

Investment Preferences

Minimum Investment:	ECU 1.5m
Preferred Investment:	ECU 1.5–10m
Type of Funding:	Equity with loan
Stage of Investment:	Expansion/Buy-out
Investment Conditions:	Profitable or very nearly profitable with stable or growing earnings
Industry Preferences:	None
Geographical Preferences:	Western Europe

Contacts:	Otto van der Wyck (Chief Executive)
	John Burgess (Director)
	Paul Griffiths (Director)

Company:	**BARNES THOMSON MANAGEMENT LIMITED**
Address:	65 New Cavendish Street, London W1M 7RD
Telephone:	01–487 3870
Telex:	27950 (Ref. 1151)
Fax:	01–436 5245

Company Details

Full-time Executives:	2
Type of Organisation:	Independent
Funds Managed:	Syntech Information Technology Fund, Syntech Information Technology Second Fund
Total Capital Invested:	£4m
Total Capital Available:	£5.5m
Specialisations:	Information technology
Current Portfolio Size:	12
Investments as	
Lead Investor:	LDR Systems; PAFEC CAE; Caplin Cybernetics Corporation; Praxis plc

Investment Preferences

Minimum Investment:	£100,000
Preferred Investment:	£300,000
Type of Funding:	Equity/Loan
Stage of Investment:	Start-up/expansion/MBO/MBI
Investment Conditions:	Strong market position with expectation of profit growth
Industry Preferences:	Solely information technology
Geographical Preferences:	UK

Contacts:	Kenneth R. Barnes, David Thomson

Company:	**BARONSMEAD PLC**
Address:	Clerkenwell House, 67 Clerkenwell Road, London EC1R 5BH
Telephone:	01–242 4900
Telex:	—
Fax:	01–242 2048

Company Details

Full-time Executives:	9
Type of Organisation:	Independent
Funds Managed:	Baronsmead Venture Capital plc and three BES Funds
Total Capital Invested:	£24m
Total Capital Available:	£29m
Specialisations:	Information technology, retail, service businesses

Current Portfolio Size:	42
Investments as	
Lead Investor:	Calidus Systems Limited; Furnitureland plc; CSE Plant Limited; John E. Wiltshier Group plc; Kaye Aluminium plc

Investment Preferences

Minimum Investment:	£250,000
Preferred Investment:	£500,000–£1m +
Type of Funding:	Mainly Equity
Stage of Investment:	All stages but particularly expansion, management buy-outs and buy-ins
Investment Conditions:	High growth potential
Industry Preferences:	Information technology, retail. All sectors but emphasis on publishing and service businesses
Geographical Preferences:	UK

Contacts:	David Wyeth, Graham Barnes

Company:	**BIRMINGHAM TECHNOLOGY (VENTURE CAPITAL) LTD**
Address:	Aston Science Park, Love Lane, Aston Triangle, Birmingham B7 4BJ
Telephone:	021–359 0981
Telex:	334535 BMTECH G
Fax:	021–359 0433

Company Details

Full-time Executives:	6
Type of Organisation:	Independent
Funds Managed:	Birmingham Technology (Venture Capital) Ltd
Total Capital Invested:	£1.1m
Total Capital Available:	£5m
Specialisations:	High growth technology companies
Current Portfolio Size:	11
Investments as	
Lead Investor:	Techsonix (UK) Ltd; AD2 Ltd; Cimtel Ltd

Investment Preferences

Minimum Investment:	£20,000

Preferred Investment:	£20,000–£250,000
	(will syndicate above)
Type of Funding:	Equity with Loan
Stage of Investment:	Seed capital and start-up
Investment Conditions:	Able to satisfy minimum rate of return
Industry Preferences:	High growth technology
Geographical Preferences:	City of Birmingham

Contacts:	Mr D.W. Harris – Director of Finance, Mr T.F.C. Crawley – Business Development Manager

Company:	**BRITISH LINEN FUND MANAGERS LIMITED**
Address:	32 Melville Street, Edinburgh EH3 7HA
Telephone:	031–243 8464
Telex:	728139
Fax:	031–243 8554

Company Details

Full-time Executives:	5
Type of Organisation:	Independent/Captive/BES
Funds Managed:	Melville Street Investments PLC
	Scottish Ventures Fund
	Second Melville Fund
	British Linen Securities
	Venture Strathclyde Fund
Total Capital Invested:	£30m
Total Capital Available:	£7m
Specialisations:	None
Current Portfolio Size:	Over 90
Investments as	
Lead Investor:	Lasalle Petroleum Services; G.A. Holdings; Highway Finance Holdings; Gleneagles Hotels PLC; Murrayfield PLC

Investment Preferences

Minimum Investment:	£100,000
Preferred Investment:	Up to £1m (UK only)
Type of Funding:	Equity only/Equity with loan
Stage of Investment:	All stages
Investment Conditions:	Flexible

Industry Preferences:	None
Geographical Preferences:	UK

Contacts:	Douglas Anderson (031–243 8463),
	Brian Finlayson (031–243 8470),
	Ewan Jeffrey (031–243 8472),
	Russell Leaker (031–243 8477)

Company:	**BRITISH TECHNOLOGY GROUP**
Address:	101 Newington Causeway, London SE1 6BU
Telephone:	01–403 6666
Telex:	894397
Fax:	01–403 7586

Company Details

Full-time Executives:	170
Type of Organisation:	Self-financing public organisation
Funds Managed:	National Research Development Corporation
Total Capital Invested:	£62m
Total Capital Available:	£25m
Specialisations:	Technological innovation
Current Portfolio Size:	170
Investments as	
Lead Investor:	—

Investment Preferences

Minimum Investment:	£50,000
Preferred Investment:	£100,000 to £1m
Type of Funding:	Equity or project funding recovered by levy on sales
Stage of Investment:	Seed Capital/Start-up/Expansion
Investment Conditions:	Must involve technological innovation
Industry Preferences:	All
Geographical Preferences:	None

Contact:	David James (Commercial Director)

Company:	**BROWN SHIPLEY DEVELOPMENT CAPITAL LTD**
Address:	Founders Court, Lothbury, London EC2R 7HE
Telephone:	01–606 9833
Telex:	886704

Fax:	01–606 9833 Extn. 3257

Company Details

Full-time Executives:	3
Type of Organisation:	Merchant Bank subsidiary managing institutional funds
Funds Managed:	Brown Shipley Development Capital Fund
Total Capital Invested:	£8m
Total Capital Available:	£16m
Specialisations:	None
Current Portfolio Size:	8
Investments as	
Lead Investor:	Trace (Computer Holdings) Ltd; Home Entertainment Corporation Ltd

Investment Preferences

Minimum Investment:	£750,000
Preferred Investment:	£1.5m
Type of Funding:	Equity
Stage of Investment:	Later stage
Investment Conditions:	High quality established businesses
Industry Preferences:	None
Geographical Preferences:	Mainly UK, will consider US & France

Contacts:	David Wills, Richard Kemp, Roy Parker

Company:	**CAMBRIDGE CAPITAL MANAGEMENT LTD**
Address:	13 Station Road, Cambridge, CB1 2JB
Telephone:	0223 312856
Telex:	—
Fax:	0223 65704

Company Details

Full-time Executives:	2
Type of Organisation:	Independent
Funds Managed:	Cambridge Capital Developments
	Cambridge Research and Innovation Limited (CRIL)
Total Capital Invested:	£2.5m
Total Capital Available:	£6.8m
Specialisations:	None

Current Portfolio Size:	6
Investments as	
Lead Investor:	Cambridge Lasers Ltd; Elles Ltd; OIS Engineering Ltd.

Investment Preferences

Minimum Investment:	£200,000 (CRIL Max £50,000)
Preferred Investment:	£250,000–£500,000
Type of Funding:	Equity only and equity with loan
Stage of Investment:	Expansion, buy-outs, buy-ins, and exceptionally replacement
Investment Conditions:	Profitability preferred
Industry Preferences:	None
Geographical Preferences:	East Anglia/East Midlands based

Contact:	Gordon Montgomery

Company:	**CANDOVER INVESTMENTS plc**
Address:	Cedric House, 8/9 East Harding Street, London EC4A 3ES
Telephone:	01–583 5090
Telex:	928035
Fax:	01–583 0717

Company Details

Full-time Executives:	7
Type of Organisation:	Public company
Funds Managed:	The Hoare Candover Exempt Fund
	The Candover 1987 Fund
	Own Funds
Total Capital Invested:	£20m
Total Capital Available:	Unlimited
Specialisations:	None
Current Portfolio Size:	35
Investments as	
Lead Investor:	Caradon plc; Technology Project Services PLC; Berkertex Holdings Ltd; Crabtree of Gateshead Ltd; Lowndes Lambert Group Ltd

Investment Preferences

Minimum Investment:	£2m

Preferred Investment:	£5m–unlimited
Type of Funding:	Equity with loan
Stage of Investment:	Buy-out
Investment Conditions:	Cash generating, proven products not subject to technological change
Industry Preferences:	None
Geographical Preferences:	None

Contacts:	C.R.E. Brooke, S.W. Curran, G.D. Fairservice

Company:	**CAPITAL PARTNERS INTERNATIONAL LTD**
Address:	Kingsmead House, 250 Kings Road, London SW3 5UE
Telephone:	01–351 4899/01–352 3159
Telex:	94012871 CAPI G
Fax:	01–376 5983

Company Details

Full-time Executives:	5
Type of Organisation:	Independent
Funds Managed:	Capital Partners International
Total Capital Invested:	—
Total Capital Available:	Open ended
Specialisations:	Assistance in overseas market introductions
Current Portfolio Size:	8
Investments as Lead Investor:	—

Investment Preferences

Minimum Investment:	No minimum
Preferred Investment:	£30,000–£300,000
Type of Funding:	Equity or Equity with loan
Stage of Investment:	All stages
Investment Conditions:	Flexible
Industry Preferences:	With global expansion potential
Geographical Preferences:	UK, Continental Europe, US, Brazil

Contact:	Dr Christoph von Luttitz, M.B.A. M.I.M.

Company:	**CAPITAL VENTURES LIMITED**
Address:	Rutherford Way, Cheltenham, Glos GL51 9TR

Telephone:	0242 584380
Telex:	—
Fax:	0242 226671

Company Details

Full-time Executives:	7
Type of Organisation:	Independent/BES/Enterprise Zone Investments
Funds Managed:	The Guinness Mahon
	Business Expansion Fund; The Arbuthnot Business Expansion Fund; The Cave Fund; The Cave 1986/87 Fund; The Capital Inn Fund
Total Capital Invested:	Over £70m
Total Capital Available:	Open ended
Specialisations:	Hotels/Property Investment
Current Portfolio Size:	60 +
Investments as	
Lead Investor:	Roman Homes PLC; Ensign Group PLC; Chester International Hotel PLC; Ashford International Hotel PLC; First Roman Property Trust PLC

Investment Preferences

Minimum Investment:	£250,000
Preferred Investment:	£500,000–No Limit
Type of Funding:	Equity with loan
Stage of Investment:	All stages
Investment Conditions:	Balanced management team with enthusiasm and commitment
Industry Preferences:	All sectors considered
Geographical Preferences:	None

Contacts:	Simon Smith, Andrew Bruckland

Company:	**CASTLEFORTH FUND MANAGERS LIMITED**
Address:	10 Charterhouse Square, London EC1M 6EH and 174 High Street, Edinburgh EH1 1QS
Telephone:	01–490 4113/031–225 2148
Telex:	—
Fax:	01–253 5636

Company Details

Full-time Executives:	4
Type of Organisation:	Independent
Funds Managed:	4 BES Approved Funds
Total Capital Invested:	£6m
Total Capital Available:	£1m +
Specialisations:	—
Current Portfolio Size:	29
Investments as	
Lead Investor:	Rolawn, Britannia Marine

Investment Preferences

Minimum Investment:	£150,000
Preferred Investment:	£250,000–£350,000
Type of Funding:	Equity
Stage of Investment:	All stages
Investment Conditions:	—
Industry Preferences:	Media, communications
Geographical Preferences:	Scotland, England

Contacts:	Donald Workman, Jock Douglas, Chris Masterson, Johnny Maxwell (Edinburgh)

Company:	**CAUSEWAY CAPITAL LIMITED**
Address:	21 Cavendish Place, London W1M 9DL
Telephone:	01–631 3073
Telex:	—
Fax:	01–631 3883

Company Details

Full-time Executives:	5
Type of Organisation:	Independent
Funds Managed:	Causeway Development Capital Fund
	Second Causeway Development Capital Fund
	Causeway Business Expansion Fund 1984/85
	Causeway Business Expansion Fund 1985/86
Total Capital Invested:	£25m
Total Capital Available:	£45m
Specialisations:	None
Current Portfolio Size:	30 +

Investments as	
Lead Investor:	Bellwinch plc; Village Green plc; Garage Equipment Maintenance Co. Ltd; Sheffield Forgemasters (Holdings) plc; Freezrite Frozen Food Centres Ltd

Investment Preferences

Minimum Investment:	£350,000
Preferred Investment:	£500,000–£2.5m
Type of Funding:	Equity or Equity and Loan
Stage of Investment:	Expansion and buy-out
Investment Conditions:	Prospect of profitable growth
Industry Preferences:	Any
Geographical Preferences:	Any within UK

Contacts:	Lionel Anthony, Ian Cameron, Andrew Joy, David Secker Walker, Geoffrey Vero

Company:	**CENTREWAY DEVELOPMENT CAPITAL LTD**
Address:	1 Victoria Square, Birmingham B1 1BD
Telephone:	021–643 3941
Telex:	337742
Fax:	021–631 3739

Company Details

Full-time Executives:	5
Type of Organisation:	Subsidiary of Industrial Corporation
Funds Managed:	Centreway I, II, III, IV, V, VI, VII
Total Capital Invested:	£15m
Total Capital Available:	Open
Specialisations:	General industrial and commercial expertise
Current Portfolio Size:	43
Investments as	
Lead Investor:	Associated Nursing Services plc; Plastiseal (uPVC) plc

Investment Preferences

Minimum Investment:	£50,000
Preferred Investment:	£250,000 upwards
Type of Funding:	Equity

Stage of Investment:	Start-up, Expansion and Buy-out
Investment Conditions:	None
Industry Preferences:	None
Geographical Preferences:	UK

Contacts:	David Chapman, John Naylor

Company:	**CHARTERHOUSE DEVELOPMENT CAPITAL LIMITED**
Address:	7 Ludgate Broadway, London EC4V 6DX
Telephone:	01–248 4000
Telex:	884276
Fax:	01–329 4252

Company Details

Full-time Executives:	30
Type of Organisation:	Owned by The Royal Bank of Scotland Group plc
Funds Managed:	Own funds
	Management Buyout Fund
	Charterhouse Business Expansion Fund Ltd (CHEF)
	Charterhouse Development Capital Fund Ltd
Total Capital Invested:	£180m
Total Capital Available:	Open
Specialisations:	None
Current Portfolio Size:	200
Investments as Lead Investor:	ARC; ASW; MFI; Argus; Crowther

Investment Preferences

Minimum Investment:	£100,000
Preferred Investment:	£500,000–£25m
Type of Funding:	Equity or Equity/Loan
Stage of Investment:	Expansion and management buyouts
Investment Conditions:	Good management, profitable
Industry Preferences:	None
Geographical Preferences:	None but principally the UK

Contacts:	Richard Duncan (London), George Shiels (Edinburgh), Bob Hilland (Manchester)

Company:	CHARTERHOUSE VENTURE FUND
Address:	10 Hertford Street, London W1Y 7DX
Telephone:	01–409 3232
Telex:	—
Fax:	01–629 2705

Company Details

Full-time Executives:	5
Type of Organisation:	Independent
Funds Managed:	Charterhouse Venture Fund
Total Capital Invested:	£12m
Total Capital Available:	£50m
Specialisations:	Healthcare, Biosciences, Environmental Management, Electronic related
Current Portfolio Size:	26
Investments as Lead Investor:	Cambridge Research Biochemicals; Rechem Environmental Services; Mercia Diagnostics; Align-Rite International; James Martin Associates

Investment Preferences

Minimum Investment:	£200,000
Preferred Investment:	£500,000
Type of Funding:	Equity
Stage of Investment:	All stages
Investment Conditions:	None
Industry Preferences:	Healthcare, biosciences, environmental management, electronic related
Geographical Preferences:	None

Contacts:	Dr John Walker, Dr Mark Scibor-Rylski, Ronald Sheldon, Humphrey Battcock, Peter Laing

Company:	CHARTFIELD & CO LIMITED
Address:	24/26 Baltic St., London EC1Y 0TB
Telephone:	01–608 1451
Telex:	—
Fax:	01–608 3158

Company Details

Full-time Executives:	6
Type of Organisation:	Independent
Funds Managed:	Chartfield Projects Ltd
	Renaissance Holdings PLC
Total Capital Invested:	£10m
Total Capital Available:	Open-ended
Specialisations:	None
Current Portfolio Size:	17
Investments as	
Lead Investor:	Advansys PLC, Munton Group PLC, Strategic Alloys Ltd

Investment Preferences:

Minimum Investment:	£100,000
Preferred Investment:	£300,000–£750,000
Type of Funding:	All types
Stage of Investment:	All stages especially recovery
Investment Conditions:	No specific conditions
Industry Preferences:	None; some excluded eg property
Geographical Preferences:	UK and USA

Contacts:	Nicholas Branch, Richard Beamiss, Andrew Collins, John Sidwell

Company:	**CIN VENTURE MANAGERS LTD**
Address:	PO Box 10, London SW1X 7AD
Telephone:	01–245 6911
Telex:	885770
Fax:	01–389 7173

Company Details

Full-time Executives:	13
Type of Organisation:	Captive
Funds Managed:	British Coal Pension Funds
	British Rail Pension Fund
Total Capital Invested:	£350m
Total Capital Available:	£100m per annum
Specialisations:	None
Current Portfolio Size:	230

Investments as
  Lead Investor: CSG; Freda Holdings; London Graphic Centre; Lindsey Holdings; Reedpack

Investment Preferences

Minimum Investment:	£250,000
Preferred Investment:	£1m +
Type of Funding:	Flexible but always an equity stake
Stage of Investment:	Start-up, expansion, buy-out, replacement
Investment Conditions:	No set parameters
Industry Preferences:	None
Geographical Preferences:	UK only

Contacts:	Robin Hall, Managing Director
	John Brown, Deputy Managing Director

Company:	**CITICORP VENTURE CAPITAL LTD**
Address:	PO Box 199, Cotton's Centre, Hay's Lane, London SE1 2QT
Telephone:	01–234 5678
Telex:	299831 CIBIL G
Fax:	01–234 2784

Company Details

Full-time Executives:	12
Type of Organisation:	Captive, Subsidiary of Citicorp
Funds Managed:	—
Total Capital Invested:	£100m
Total Capital Available:	Not limited
Specialisations:	MBO's/MBI's or larger development capital situations
Current Portfolio Size:	60 +

Investments as
  Lead Investor: TIP, Technitron; UNS, RHP Rimoldi

Investment Preferences

Minimum Investment:	£500,000
Preferred Investment:	£1m upwards
Type of Funding:	Equity and loan
Stage of Investment:	Expansion, MBO, MBI

Investment Conditions:	None
Industry Preferences:	None
Geographical Preferences:	Europe

Contact:	Michael Smith, Managing Director

Company:	**CLOSE INVESTMENT MANAGEMENT LIMITED**
Address:	36 Great St Helen's, London EC3A 6AP
Telephone:	01–283 2241
Telex:	8814274
Fax:	01–626 4487

Company Details

Full-time Executives:	8
Type of Organisation:	Independent
Funds Managed:	Close Investment 1988 Fund
	Close Investment 1986 Fund
	Close Investment 1984 Fund
Total Capital Invested:	£25m
Total Capital Available:	£55m
Specialisations:	None
Current Portfolio Size:	30
Investments as	
Lead Investor:	Crown Industrial Group Ltd; The Headland Group plc; Sheppard Moscow & Associates Ltd; Systems Offices Group Ltd; Unit Group plc

Investment Preferences

Minimum Investment:	£300,000
Preferred Investment:	£750,000–£2m
Type of Funding:	Equity and unsecured loans
Stage of Investment:	Mainly expansion and buy-out; some buy-in, early stage
Investment Conditions:	Minimum sales of £2m preferred
Industry Preferences:	None
Geographical Preferences:	UK

Contacts:	Jonathan Thornton, Jeremy Gough, John Snook, Mark Weston

Company:	**CLYDESDALE BANK EQUITY LIMITED**
Address:	30 St Vincent Place, Glasgow G1 2HL
Telephone:	041 248 7070
Telex:	77135
Fax:	041 204 0828

Company Details

Full-time Executives:	4
Type of Organisation:	Captive
Funds Managed:	—
Total Capital Invested:	£3m
Total Capital Available:	Open
Specialisations:	—
Current Portfolio Size:	15
Investments as	
Lead Investor:	—

Investment Preferences

Minimum Investment:	£100,000
Preferred Investment:	£200,000–£500,000
Type of Funding:	Mainly equity
Stage of Investment:	—
Investment Conditions:	—
Industry Preferences:	All considered
Geographical Preferences:	UK but mainly Scottish based

Contacts:	Alisdair A. Stewart, Neil J. Kennedy

Company:	**CONSOLIDATED CREDITS INVESTMENT CAPITAL**
Address:	West World, West Gate, London W5 1DT
Telephone:	01–991 2551
Telex:	8812983 CHELSI
Fax:	01–991 5263

Company Details

Full-time Executives:	3
Type of Organisation:	Independent
Funds Managed:	—

Total Capital Invested:	£5m
Total Capital Available:	As required
Specialisations:	Retailing, Travel, Hotels, Leisure, Low Technology Industry, Property
Current Portfolio Size:	10
Investments as Lead Investor:	—

Investment Preferences

Minimum Investment:	£50,000
Preferred Investment:	£100,000–£500,000
Type of Funding:	Equity, Equity & Loan Packages
Stage of Investment:	Expansion (flexible)
Investment Conditions:	Profitable, well managed companies
Industry Preferences:	Retailing, Travel & Leisure, Low Tech, Property related
Geographical Preferences:	None

Contacts:	C. Lewis, J. Lewis

Company:	**COUNTY NATWEST VENTURES LIMITED**
Address:	Drapers Gardens, 12 Throgmorton Avenue, London EC2P 2ES
Telephone:	01–382 1000
Telex:	882121
Fax:	01–638 1615

Company Details

Full-time Executives:	22 in London, 5 in Birmingham, 4 in Manchester, 5 in Leeds
Type of Organisation:	Captive
Funds Managed:	County NatWest Ventures Limited; (BES funds closed) – County 1st, 2nd and 3rd Business Expansion Funds
Total Capital Invested:	£100m + £5.2m BES
Total Capital Available:	Unlimited
Specialisations:	General
Current Portfolio Size:	231
Investments as Lead Investor:	Aynsley; Aqualisa; Magnus Developments; Holliday Chemical Holdings

Investment Preferences

Minimum Investment:	£250,000
Preferred Investment:	£500,000–£2m
Type of Funding:	Equity and Mezzanine Finance
Stage of Investment:	Expansion, buy-out, buy-in
Investment Conditions:	Strong management team. Excellent prospects for profitable growth
Industry Preferences:	None
Geographical Preferences:	UK/Europe/USA

Contacts:	D.R. Shaw – Managing Director,
	Also in London: C. McCann, S.M. Donald, P.M. Smaill, P. Bulmer
	Manchester: J. Moran
	Leeds: G. Dewhirst
	Birmingham: K.G. White

Company:	**CREDITANSTALT DEVELOPMENT CAPITAL**
Address:	29 Gresham Street, London EC2V 7AH
Telephone:	01–822 2600
Telex:	894612
Fax:	01–822 2644/2663

Company Details

Full-time Executives:	3
Type of Organisation:	Financial Institution
Funds Managed:	None
Total Capital Invested:	Approx. £15m
Total Capital Available:	No limit
Specialisations:	Medium MBO/MBIs
Current Portfolio Size:	21
Investments as Lead Investor:	—

Investment Preferences

Minimum Investment:	Equity £0.5m
	Debt £2m (Senior/Mezzanine)
Preferred Investment:	Equity £0.25m–£0.5m or
	Debt over £2m

Type of Funding:	Equity or Debt
Stage of Investment:	MBO/MBI Expansion
Investment Conditions:	3 year trading results
Industry Preferences:	None
Geographical Preferences:	None

Contacts:	Anthony G. Shayle (Manager)
	Barrie H. Moore (Assistant Director)

Company:	DARTINGTON & CO. SECURITIES LIMITED
Address:	Bush House, 70 Prince Street,
	Bristol BS1 4QD
Telephone:	0272 213206
Telex:	—
Fax:	0272 230379

Company Details

Full-time Executives:	4
Type of Organisation:	Independent
Funds Managed:	Avon Enterprise Fund & Capital West
Total Capital Invested:	£1.75m–Avon Enterprise Fund
Total Capital Available:	£2.1m–Avon Enterprise Fund
	Unlimited–Capital West
Specialisations:	None
Current Portfolio Size:	30
Investments as	
Lead Investor:	—

Investment Preferences

Minimum Investment:	£100,000–Avon Enterprise Fund
	£500,000–Capital West
Preferred Investment:	£1000,000–£2000,000–
	Avon Enterprise Fund
	£2m upwards–Capital West
Type of Funding:	Equity & Loan
Stage of Investment:	Expansion/MBO/MBI
Investment Conditions:	Profitable
Industry Preferences:	None
Geographical Preferences:	South West of England

Contact:	Sue Watson

Company:	**DCC VENTURES LIMITED**
Address:	103 Mount Street, London W1Y 5HE
Telephone:	01–491 0767
Telex:	—
Fax:	01–499 1952

Company Details

Full-time Executives:	4 UK & 14 Ireland
Type of Organisation:	Independent Limited Company with major institutional shareholders
Funds Managed:	—
Total Capital Invested:	£90m
Total Capital Available:	Open
Specialisations:	Distribution, IT, healthcare and services
Current Portfolio Size:	45
Investments as	
Lead Investor:	Fll-Fyffes plc; Flogas plc; Wardell Roberts plc; Printech International plc; Devonshire Group plc

Investment Preferences

Minimum Investment:	£250,000
Preferred Investment:	£750,000–£2,500,000
Type of Funding:	Equity or Equity Instrument
Stage of Investment:	Preferred: Expansion, Replacement, Buy-out, Buy-in
	Exceptionally: Start-up, Turnaround
Investment Conditions:	Profitable growing companies
Industry Preferences:	None
Geographical Preferences:	UK and Ireland

Contacts:	Jim Flavin, Tony Mullins, Tommy Breen

Company:	**DEVELOPMENT CAPITAL GROUP LIMITED**
Address:	44 Baker Street, London W1M 1DH
Telephone:	01–935 2731
Telex:	25247 DEVCAP
Fax:	01–935 9831

Company Details

Full-time Executives:	24

Type of Organisation:	Subsidiary of Lazard Brothers & Co. Limited, managing institutional and corporate backed funds and BES funds
Funds Managed:	The Lazard Development Capital Funds (BES); Baker Street Investment Company PLC (BASIC); The Lazard Leisure, Defence, Medical and Food & Drink Funds; The Pearson Media Development Fund; The Lazard Unquoted Companies Fund; The Welsh Venture Capital Fund; Unquoted investments held by: The Eastern Counties, North West, Ridings, Northumbria and West Midlands Regional Unit Trusts
Total Capital Invested:	Approx £65m
Total Capital Available:	In excess of £50m
Specialisations:	General, plus those sectors covered by specialist funds as listed above
Current Portfolio Size:	120
Investments as Lead Investor:	Radamec, Logitek, Magnetic Materials Group, Doeflex

Investment Preferences

Minimum Investment:	£250,000
Preferred Investment:	£750,000–£2m
Type of Funding:	Equity only/Equity with Loan
Stage of Investment:	Start-up/Expansion/Buy-out
Investment Conditions:	Good growth prospects, sound management
Industry Preferences:	All sectors considered
Geographical Preferences:	UK

Contacts:	Tom Glucklich, Douglas Hudson, Charles Cox, Richard Bowes, Anthony Denham, Mark Hawkesworth

Company:	**EAGLE STAR INVESTMENT MANAGERS LTD**
Address:	60, St. Mary Axe, London EC3A 8JQ
Telephone:	01–929 1111
Telex:	914962
Fax:	01–626 1266

Company Details

Full-time Executives:	2
Type of Organisation:	Venture Capital Unit within E.S.I.M., a subsidiary of Eagle Star Insurance Co.
Funds Managed:	Eagle Star Insurance Co. Ltd
Total Capital Invested:	£60m
Total Capital Available:	Open
Specialisations:	None
Current Portfolio Size:	35
Investments as Lead Investor:	—

Investment Preferences

Minimum Investment:	£250,000
Preferred Investment:	£250,000–£5m
Type of Funding:	Flexible
Stage of Investment:	All stages
Investment Conditions:	None
Industry Preferences:	All sectors considered
Geographical Preferences:	UK, Europe, USA

Contacts:	Carol Ames, Keku Aga

Company:	**ECI VENTURES**
Address:	Brettenham House, Lancaster Place, London WC2E 7EN
Telephone:	01–606 1000
Telex:	—
Fax:	01–240 5050

Company Details

Full-time Executives:	12
Type of Organisation:	Independent
Funds Managed:	ECI Investments
	Equity Capital Unit Trust
	ECI International Partnership
	ECI International Trust
	ECI Developments

Total Capital Invested:	£70m
Total Capital Available:	£50m
Specialisations:	General
Current Portfolio Size:	95
Investments as	
Lead Investor:	Bloomsbury Publishing; Equator; Straker; J.W. Wiltshier

Investment Preferences

Minimum Investment:	£350,000
Preferred Investment:	£1m–£5m
Type of Funding:	Primarily Equity
Stage of Investment:	Expansion, Buy-outs, Buy-ins
Investment Conditions:	Management track record. Realisable in 5–7 years
Industry Preferences:	All sectors including technology
Geographical Preferences:	UK, selected Continental/USA
Contacts:	Tony Lorenz, David Wansbrough, Jonathan Baker, Stephen Dawson, Martin Makey, Ian Salkeld, Roger Hay, Paul Thomas, Ken Landsberg, Paul Jobson, Jeremy Ellison

Company:	**ELECTRA INNVOTEC LIMITED**
Address:	65 Kingsway, London WC2B 6QT
Telephone:	01–831 9901
Telex:	265525
Fax:	01–240 8565

Company Details

Full-time Executives:	4
Type of Organisation:	Independent
Funds Managed:	Electra Innvotec Limited Partnership
Total Capital Invested:	£2.2m
Total Capital Available:	£18.4m
Specialisations:	Corporate venturing, manufacturing
Current Portfolio Size:	5
Investments as	
Lead Investor:	BFR Limited, Transon Heat Engineering plc, Industrial Friction International Ltd.

Investment Preferences

Minimum Investment:	£300,000
Preferred Investment:	£1m
Type of Funding:	Equity
Stage of Investment:	Start-up expansion
Investment Conditions:	None
Industry Preferences:	All manufacturing, manufacturing related
Geographical Preferences:	UK

Contacts: Peter Dohrn, Malcolm Malir, Alan Mawson, Hugh Stewart

Company:	**ELECTRA KINGSWAY LIMITED**
Address:	65 Kingsway, London WC2B 6QT
Telephone:	01–831 6464
Telex:	265525 ELECG G
Fax:	01–404 5388

Company Details

Full-time Executives:	20
Type of Organisation:	Independent
Funds Managed:	Electra Investment Trust plc
	Electra Private Equity Partners
Total Capital Invested:	£388m
Total Capital Available:	In excess of £350m
Specialisations:	None
Current Portfolio Size:	200
Investments as	
Lead Investor:	U.K. Paper; BPCC; Aviation Holdings; Sphere Drake; Humberclyde Investments; Unipart

Investment Preferences

Minimum Investment:	£1m
Preferred Investment:	£2–£20m
Type of Funding:	All types of equity and mezzanine
Stage of Investment:	All stages
Investment Conditions:	None
Industry Preferences:	None
Geographical Preferences:	UK, Continental Europe and USA

Contacts:	Robert Drummond, Hugh Mumford, David Osborne, David Symondson (Directors), Jonathan Bond, Robert Clarke, Rowan Gormley, Oliver Huntsman, Julian Knott, Peter Rowledge, Paddy Sandford-Johnson, Tim Syder

Company:	**E.M. WARBURG, PINCUS & CO. INTERNATIONAL LIMITED**
Address:	20 St James's Street, London SW1A 1ES
Telephone:	01–321 0129
Telex:	94017686
Fax:	01–321 0881

Company Details

Full-time Executives:	3 in London (45 professionals in total, mainly in New York)
Type of Organisation:	Independent, a subsidiary of E.M. Warburg, Pincus & Co. Inc.
Funds Managed:	Warburg Pincus Capital Company LP Warburg Pincus Capital Partners LP Warburg Pincus Associates LP
Total Capital Invested:	£680m (in four funds)
Total Capital Available:	£315m (in most recent fund)
Specialisations:	Media, Entertainment, Retail Distribution, Medical, Life Sciences, Health Care
Current Portfolio Size:	30 (most recent fund)
Investments as Lead Investor:	Christians Int'l, Centaur Communications Ltd; Ingersoll Publishing Ltd

Investment Preferences

Minimum Investment:	£2m
Preferred Investment:	£5–£20m
Type of Funding:	Mainly equity plus mezzanine when required
Stage of Investment:	Preference for 'Special Situations' (buy-outs, buy-ins, recapitalisations, etc.) and expansion stage venture financings
Investment Conditions:	No special conditions
Industry Preferences:	None
Geographical Preferences:	UK and Continental Europe

Contacts:	A. Michael Hoffman (Managing Director)
	Barbara L. Manfrey (Managing Director)

Company:	**EUROCONTINENTAL (ADVISERS) LTD**
Address:	4–6 Throgmorton Avenue, London EC2N 2AP
Telephone:	01–638 6111
Telex:	—
Fax:	01–588 4763

Company Details

Full-time Executives:	5
Type of Organisation:	Subsidiary of Credit Agricole, D.G. Bank and Management
Funds Managed:	Eurocontinental Ventures S.A.
Total Capital Invested:	ECU 6.6m
Total Capital Available:	ECU 26.4m
Specialisations:	European family re-alignment situations; 1992 redeployment opportunities
Current Portfolio Size:	13
Investments as Lead Investor:	SOFDIT (France)

Investment Preferences

Minimum Investment:	ECU 300,000 (£200,000)
Preferred Investment:	ECU 900,000 (£600,000)
Type of Funding:	Equity
Stage of Investment:	Expansion and development finance, MBO, MBI
Investment Conditions:	Established businesses with growth potential
Industry Preferences:	All sectors including developed technology
Geographical Preferences:	Right across EEC and Europe

Contacts:	Minoo Randeria, Albert Gabizon, Pascal Brandys, Deyman Eastmond, Peter Abbott

Company:	**FLEMING VENTURES LTD**
Address:	World Trade Centre, International House, 1 St Katherine's Way, London E1 9UN
Telephone:	01–480 6211
Telex:	—
Fax:	01–481 1156

Company Details

Full-time Executives:	3
Type of Organisation:	Affiliated to Robert Fleming & Co.
Funds Managed:	Fleming Ventures Ltd
Total Capital Invested:	£10.26m
Total Capital Available:	c. £8m
Specialisations:	Electronics
Current Portfolio Size:	20
Investments as	
Lead Investor:	Disc Technology Ltd; Ferranti Creditphone Ltd; Industrial Systems Solutions Ltd; IP Test Ltd

Investment Preferences

Minimum Investment:	£250,000
Preferred Investment:	£500,000
Type of Funding:	Equity
Stage of Investment:	Startups/Later Stage/MBOs
Investment Conditions:	Profitable unless special circumstances (e.g. Government license)
Industry Preferences:	High Technology/Electronics
Geographical Preferences:	UK & USA

Contacts:	Peter English, Bernard Fairman

Company:	**FOREIGN & COLONIAL VENTURES LIMITED**
Address:	6 Laurence Pountney Hill, London EC4R 0BA
Telephone:	01–782 9829
Telex:	886197
Fax:	01–626 4947

Company Details

Full-time Executives:	7
Type of Organisation:	Captive
Funds Managed:	F. & C. Ventures Limited Partnership
	F. & C. Enterprise Trust PLC
	F. & C. Buy-out Trust Limited
	Clients of Foreign & Colonial Management Limited

Total Capital Invested:	£60m
Total Capital Available:	£80m
Specialisations:	None
Current Portfolio Size:	100
Investments as	
Lead Investor:	The Art Group; Computacenter; Essanelle; First Mortgage Securities; Speciality Shops

Investment Preferences

Minimum Investment:	£500,000
Preferred Investment:	£500,000–£3m
Type of Funding:	Equity
Stage of Investment:	Development and MBO/MBI
Investment Conditions:	Turnover of £1,000,000
Industry Preferences:	None
Geographical Preferences:	UK & Northern Europe

Contacts:	The Hon James Nelson, Mark Fane, Rod Richards, Michael Boxford, William Eccles, Marcus Hawkins (London), Robin Peters (Leeds)

Company:	**GARTMORE INVESTMENT LIMITED**
Address:	Gartmore House, 16–18 Monument Street, London EC3R 8AJ
Telephone:	01–623 1212
Telex:	888606 GAFUND G
Fax:	01–283 6070

Company Details

Full-time Executives:	3
Type of Organisation:	Independent
Funds Managed:	English & Caledonian Investment PLC
	London & Strathclyde Trust PLC
	English & Scottish Investors PLC
Total Capital Invested:	£20m
Total Capital Available:	£50m
Specialisations:	None
Current Portfolio Size:	50
Investments as	
Lead Investor:	Ashtead Plant; Video Tape Recording; G & F Retail

Investment Preferences

Minimum Investment:	£250,000
Preferred Investment:	£500,000–£2m
Type of Funding:	Equity and loan
Stage of Investment:	Expansion, MBO/MBI
Investment Conditions:	None
Industry Preferences:	None
Geographical Preferences:	UK, USA, Europe

Contacts:	Michael Walton, Douglas Abbott, Graham Walden

Company:	**GLOBE MANAGEMENT LIMITED**
Address:	Globe House, 4 Temple Place, London WC2R 3HP
Telephone:	01–836 7766
Telex:	24101
Fax:	01–836 6129

Company Details

Full-time Executives:	5
Type of Organisation:	Independent
Funds Managed:	Globe Investment Trust PLC
Total Capital Invested:	£165m
Total Capital Available:	Open
Specialisations:	None
Current Portfolio Size:	85
Investments as Lead Investor:	Derby International Corporation

Investment Preferences

Minimum Investment:	£1m
Preferred Investment:	£3m–£5m
Type of Funding:	Equity only or equity with loan
Stage of Investment:	Selected start-ups, management buy-outs, development capital
Investment Conditions:	None
Industry Preferences:	All considered
Geographical Preferences:	UK, Europe and North America

Contacts:	Jimmy West (Managing Director), David Gregson, Hugh Lenon, John Short, Anne Wolff

Company:	**GRANVILLE & CO. LIMITED**
Address:	Mint House, 77 Mansell Street, London E1 8AF
Telephone:	01–488 1212
Telex:	8814884 GVILCO G
Fax:	01–481 3911

Company Details

Full-time Executives:	10
Type of Organisation:	Independent
Funds Managed:	Granville Venture Capital
	Granville Modern Management Trust
	Callander Granville Euromanagement Fund
Total Capital Invested:	£40m
Total Capital Available:	£80m
Specialisations:	None
Current Portfolio Size:	25
Investments as	
Lead Investor:	Serco Group, PLC; Ritz Design; Sanitan; Haigh Castle; Sirex Europe BV; Interaccess BV

Investment Preferences

Minimum Investment:	£200,000
Preferred Investment:	£250,000–£6m
Type of Funding:	Flexible but always an equity stake
Stage of Investment:	All stages
Investment Conditions:	None
Industry Preferences:	None
Geographical Preferences:	UK and Europe

Contacts:	Michael Proudlock, David Steeds, Guy Eastman, David Hemming, Charles Thompson, Chris Lane, Diane Kneip, Alison Ridge

Company:	**GREATER LONDON ENTERPRISE**
Address:	63–67 Newington Causeway, London SE1 6BD
Telephone:	01–403 0300
Telex:	896616 SENDIT G
Fax:	01–403 1742

Company Details

Full-time Executives:	13 investment executives across the Greater London Enterprise Group
Type of Organisation:	Public investment business
Funds Managed:	London Enterprise Venture Fund (LEVF) plus our funds
Total Capital Invested:	£4m at 31 July 1988
Total Capital Available:	£7m at 31 July 1988
Specialisations:	Diverse
Current Portfolio Size:	15 equity investments at 31 July 1988
Investments as	
Lead Investor:	Flux Ltd; Multiform Concrete Ltd; Progress International Ltd; Theatre Projects Consultants Ltd

Investment Preferences

Minimum Investment:	£40,000
Preferred Investment:	Within range of £40,000 to £500,000
Type of Funding:	Equity
Stage of Investment:	Various, from pre start-up to MBO
Investment Conditions:	Close involvement in trustee companies
Industry Preferences:	None
Geographical Preferences:	Greater London area

Contact:	Richard Minns, Joint Chief Executive

Company:	**GREATER MANCHESTER ECONOMIC DEVELOPMENT LIMITED**
Address:	Bernard House, Piccadilly Gardens, Manchester M1 4DD
Telephone:	061–236 4412
Telex:	665770 GMEDC G
Fax:	061–228 6462

Company Details

Full-time Executives:	4
Type of Organisation:	Independent, responsible to Greater Manchester District Councils
Funds Managed:	—
Total Capital Invested:	£3m +

Total Capital Available:	£3m +
Specialisations:	—
Current Portfolio Size:	40
Investments as Lead Investor:	—

Investment Preferences

Minimum Investment:	£25,000
Preferred Investment:	£25,000–£250,000 +
Type of Funding:	Equity and loan
Stage of Investment:	Start-up, expansion, buy-out
Investment Conditions:	—
Industry Preferences:	Manufacturing & productive service industries
Geographical Preferences:	Greater Manchester

Contacts:	Ian Bolton

Company:	**GRESHAM TRUST p.l.c.**
Address:	Barrington House, Gresham Street, London EC2V 7HE
Telephone:	01–606 6474
Telex:	887153
Fax:	01–606 3370

Company Details

Full-time Executives:	7
Type of Organisation:	Captive, BES
Funds Managed:	Gresham Trust Business Expansion Funds 1984/85 and 1985/86; Gresham Trust Management Buy-Out BES Fund
Total Capital Invested:	£13m
Total Capital Available:	Open
Specialisations:	None
Current Portfolio Size:	68
Investments as Lead Investor:	Senior Secretaries Limited; A & J Bull Limited; Skyway Group PLC; Tiphook Plc; HunterPrint Group Plc

Investment Preferences

Minimum Investment:	£250,000

Preferred Investment:	£500,000
Type of Funding:	Equity or Equity and Preference Shares
Stage of Investment:	Expansion, buy-out, buy-in, share purchase
Investment Conditions:	Quality management and growth prospects
Industry Preferences:	None
Geographical Preferences:	Within UK

| Contacts: | Tony Diment, Trevor Jones, David Ascott, Mike Thornton |

Company:	**GROSVENOR VENTURE MANAGERS LIMITED**
Address:	Commerce House, 2–6 Bath Road, Slough, Berkshire SL1 3RZ
Telephone:	0753 32623
Telex:	848314 CHACOM G
Fax:	0753 34879

Company Details

Full-time Executives:	8
Type of Organisation:	Independent
Funds Managed:	Grosvenor Development Capital
	Grosvenor Technology Fund
	Third Grosvenor Fund
Total Capital Invested:	£25m
Total Capital Available:	£42m
Specialisations:	Technology based companies
Current Portfolio Size:	40 current plus 28 realised
Investments as	
Lead Investor:	Electron House; Marcol Group; Hayes Shell Cast; ACT Computer Services; Sage Group

Investment Preferences

Minimum Investment:	£200,000
Preferred Investment:	£500,000–£1.5m
Type of Funding:	Equity and Equity with loan
Stage of Investment:	Expansion, Replacement Capital, Buy-outs
Investment Conditions:	Preferably PBT £100,000
Industry Preferences:	None
Geographical Preferences:	Preferably UK

Contacts:	David Beattie, Ian Taylor, Michael Glover, Gavan Sellers, Janis Anderson

Company:	**GUINNESS MAHON DEVELOPMENT CAPITAL LTD**
Address:	32 St Mary at Hill, London EC3P 3AJ
Telephone:	01–623 9333
Telex:	884035
Fax:	01–626 7007

Company Details

Full-time Executives:	4
Type of Organisation:	Venture Capital subsidiary of listed financial services group
Funds Managed:	The London Development Capital Fund Ltd
	2 BES Schemes
Total Capital Invested:	£10m
Total Capital Available:	No specific limit
Specialisations:	Medical, Buy-ins, Expansion
Current Portfolio Size:	38
Investments as	
Lead Investor:	Godfrey Cave Holdings; Tower Bridge Holdings; Emeritus Corporation; Mobilia; Reece

Investment Preferences

Minimum Investment:	£50,000
Preferred Investment:	£500,000
Type of Funding:	As appropriate
Stage of Investment:	Expansion, buy-ins, early stage only in medical and bioscience sectors
Investment Conditions:	None
Industry Preferences:	Medical for Medical Fund, otherwise none
Geographical Preferences:	London for London Development Capital Fund, otherwise none

Contacts:	G.R. Power – Managing Director
	M.K.H.M. Moss – Executive
	W.J. Lambert – Executive

Company:	(GPI) GYLLENHAMMAR & PARTNERS INTERNATIONAL LTD
Address:	Little Tufton House, 3 Dean Trench Street, London SW1P 3HB
Telephone:	01–222 8151
Telex:	914024
Fax:	01–222 0893

Company Details

Full-time Executives:	6
Type of Organisation:	Independent partnership with a Swedish Investment Banking Group
Funds Managed:	G.P.O., I.S.I.C., G.D.C.
Total Capital Invested:	£10m
Total Capital Available:	£15m
Specialisations:	Mature industries, restructuring
Current Portfolio Size:	9
Investments as Lead Investor:	—

Investment Preferences

Minimum Investment:	£500,000
Preferred Investment:	£2m
Type of Funding:	Equity/Mezzanine
Stage of Investment:	Expansion/Restructuring
Investment Conditions:	High profit/growth potential
Industry Preferences:	Mature industries
Geographical Preferences:	UK & Europe

Contacts:	Dr Lars Ahrell, James Walton

Company:	HAMBROS ADVANCED TECHNOLOGY TRUST PLC
Address:	20/21 Tooks Court, Cursitor Street, London EC4A 1LB
Telephone:	01–242 9900
Telex:	23849 TOPHAT
Fax:	01–405 2863

Company Details

Full-time Executives:	6
Type of Organisation:	Independent
Funds Managed:	Hambros Advanced Technology Trust PLC
	Adviser to: KKI-Hambro European International Venture Fund
Total Capital Invested:	£9.3m
Total Capital Available:	£4.8m
Specialisations:	Telecommunications, information technology, software, medical electronics
Current Portfolio Size:	38
Investments as Lead Investor:	Appleton Ultrasound Ltd; Procal Analytics Ltd

Investment Preferences

Minimum Investment:	£100,000
Preferred Investment:	£250,000
Type of Funding:	Equity only
Stage of Investment:	Start-up/Expansion
Investment Conditions:	None
Industry Preferences:	High Technology
Geographical Preferences:	UK, Continental Europe, USA

Contacts:	Harry Fitzgibbons, Managing Director; Jamie Weir, Director

Company:	**HAMBRO EUROPEAN VENTURES LIMITED**
Address:	41 Tower Hill, London EC3N 4HA
Telephone:	01-480 5000
Telex:	883851
Fax:	01-702 9827

Company Details

Full-time Executives:	5
Type of Organisation:	Captive
Funds Managed:	Hambro European Ventures Partnership
Total Capital Invested:	£2.5m
Total Capital Available:	£14m, more in certain circumstances
Specialisations:	Financial, Publishing, Property and Manufacturing

Current Portfolio Size:	7
Investments as	
Lead Investor:	MBM; Bernerwerke

Investment Preferences

Minimum Investment:	£250,000
Preferred Investment:	£500,000–£1m
Type of Funding:	Equity and subordinated debt
Stage of Investment:	MBO's, MBI's, refinancing, development
Investment Conditions:	No special conditions
Industry Preferences:	Not high technology start-ups – See Hambros Advanced Technology Trust
Geographical Preferences:	UK & Europe

Contacts:	Gilbert Chalk, Nicholas Page, Edmund Truell, Anthony Mallin, Carter Siebens

Company:	**HILL SAMUEL DEVELOPMENT CAPITAL**
Address:	100 Wood Street, London EC2P 2AJ
Telephone:	01–628 8011
Telex:	888822
Fax:	01–588 5281

Company Details

Full-time Executives:	9
Type of Organisation:	Development Capital Funds managed by Hill Samuel Bank Ltd.
Funds Managed:	First Fountain Development Capital Fund Second Fountain Development Capital Fund TSB/Hill Samuel
Total Capital Invested:	£11.5m
Total Capital Available:	Unlimited
Specialisations:	None
Current Portfolio Size:	20
Investments as	
Lead Investor:	Corroless International Ltd; Hinari Consumer Electronics Ltd; Kingsgrange plc; NFI Group Ltd

Investment Preferences

Minimum Investment:	£250,000
Preferred Investment:	£250,000–£2m

Type of Funding:	Equity and Loan Capital
Stage of Investment:	Expansion, MBO/MBI, replacement capital
Investment Conditions:	None
Industry Preferences:	None
Geographical Preferences:	UK

Contacts:	Garry Watson, Philip Williams, Kevin Wilkinson, Richard Ramsey, Yagnish Chotai, Simon Ffitch, Andrew Fullerton, Mike Walker

Company:	**HODGSON MARTIN LIMITED**
Address:	36 George Street, Edinburgh EH2 2LE
Telephone:	031–226 7644
Telex:	727039
Fax:	031–226 7647

Company Details

Full-time Executives:	5
Type of Organisation:	Independent
Funds Managed:	The Northern Venture Capital Syndicates
	Abbey BES Syndicates
	St Andrew Syndicates
Total Capital Invested:	£10m
Total Capital Available:	Open
Specialisations:	None
Current Portfolio Size:	52
Investments as	
Lead Investor:	Stuart Wyse Ogilvie (Estates); Wharfside Hotels PLC; Beechwood Scotland Limited; KDM International; North West Times

Investment Preferences

Minimum Investment:	£150,000
Preferred Investment:	£250,000
Type of Funding:	Equity only
Stage of Investment:	Start-up/Expansion/Buy-out
Investment Conditions:	Flexible
Industry Preferences:	None
Geographical Preferences:	UK

Contacts:	Allan Hodgson, Sheila Mackie, Lindsay Boyd, Yvonne Savage

Company:	3i plc
Address:	91 Waterloo Road, London SE1 8XP
Telephone:	01–928 7822
Telex:	917844
Fax:	01–928 0058

Company Details

Full-time Executives:	750
Type of Organisation:	Independent-unquoted public company
Funds Managed:	None
Total Capital Invested:	£4bn
Total Capital Available:	Unlimited
Specialisations:	All industry sectors
Current Portfolio Size:	5,000
Investments as Lead Investor:	Travellers Fare; Exacta Circuits Ltd; M4 Data Ltd

Investment Preferences

Minimum Investment:	All sizes
Preferred Investment:	£100,000–£50m
Type of Funding:	Equity only and Equity with loan as appropriate
Stage of Investment:	Seed, Start-up, Expansion, Buy-out, Buy-in. Expertise in funding and advice to businesses of all sizes from hands on early stage support through all phases of business growth and restructuring
Investment Conditions:	Flexible investment packages to suit all situations
Industry Preferences:	All sectors
Geographical Preferences:	UK, EEC, USA

Contacts:	Paul Waller, Eric Barton, Geoff Taylor or any 3i office

Company:	IC INVESTMENT MANAGEMENT LIMITED
Address:	1 Adam Street, London WC2N 6AW
Telephone:	01–930 1262
Telex:	22497 ICINSC G
Fax:	01–839 7479

Company Details

Full-time Executives:	1
Type of Organisation:	In-house Venture/Development Capital, Captive Fund
Funds Managed:	Imperial Chemical Industries Pension Funds
Total Capital Invested:	£7m
Total Capital Available:	Open-ended
Specialisations:	General
Current Portfolio Size:	5 in UK
Investments as Lead Investor:	—

Investment Preferences:

Minimum Investment:	£750,000
Preferred Investment:	£750,000–£3m
Type of Funding:	Equity or Equity/Loan
Stage of Investment:	Expansion, Replacement Capital, Buy-outs
Investment Conditions:	Not rescue, preferably profitable, realisable within 5 years
Industry Preferences:	None
Geographical Preferences:	UK

Contact:	Jeremy Coller

Company:	**INDUSTRIAL DEVELOPMENT BOARD FOR NORTHERN IRELAND**
Address:	IDB House, 64 Chichester Street, Belfast BT1 4JX
Telephone:	0232 233233
Telex:	747025
Fax:	0232 231328

Company Details

Full-time Executives:	11
Type of Organisation:	Government sponsored
Funds Managed:	—
Total Capital Invested:	£6.6m as at 31.3.88
Total Capital Available:	Open
Specialisations:	—
Current Portfolio Size:	39

Investments as
  Lead Investor: —

Investment Preferences

Minimum Investment: None
Preferred Investment: Open
Type of Funding: Equity and loan
Stage of Investment: —
Investment Conditions: —
Industry Preferences: Manufacturing & Tradeable Services
Geographical Preferences: Northern Ireland

Contact: Mr. C.S.A. Harding

Company: **INDUSTRIAL TECHNOLOGY SECURITIES LIMITED**
Address: Omega House, 6 Buckingham Place, Bellfield Road, High Wycombe, Bucks HP13 5HW
Telephone: 0494 459923
Telex: —
Fax: 0494 459543

Company Details

Full-time Executives: 2
Type of Organisation: BES Fund Manager
Funds Managed: 1984/85 Industrial Technology Fund
1985/86 Industrial Technology Fund
1986/87 Industrial Technology Fund
The Fourth Industrial Technology Fund
Total Capital Invested: £3.5m
Total Capital Available: —
Specialisations: Industrial Technology Companies
Current Portfolio Size: 20
Investments as
  Lead Investor: —

Investment Preferences

Minimum Investment: £150,000
Preferred Investment: £250,000
Type of Funding: BES Equity only

Stage of Investment:	Start-up, Expansion
Investment Conditions:	Good management; high gross margins; defendable market position
Industry Preferences:	Technology based companies
Geographical Preferences:	UK

Contacts:	Jon Berglund, Michael Cohen

Company:	**IVORY & SIME DEVELOPMENT CAPITAL**
Address:	One Charlotte Square, Edinburgh EH2 4DZ
Telephone:	031–225 1357
Telex:	727242 IVORYS G
Fax:	031–225 2375

Company Details

Full-time Executives:	4
Type of Organisation:	Independent
Funds Managed:	The Independent Investment Company PLC London American Ventures Trust PLC 5 quoted investment trusts managed by Ivory & Sime plc
Total Capital Invested:	£130m
Total Capital Available:	£170m
Specialisations:	General
Current Portfolio Size:	120
Investments as	
Lead Investor:	American Healthcare; Bankside; Cumberland Natural Gas; Needwood Holdings; Wharfedale

Investment Preferences

Minimum Investment:	£150,000
Preferred Investment:	Over £1m
Type of Funding:	Equity or Equity related
Stage of Investment:	Mainly development/MBO/MBI
Investment Conditions:	None
Industry Preferences:	None
Geographical Preferences:	UK, Europe, USA

Contacts:	Mark Tyndall, Richard Muir-Simpson, Andy Steel

Company:	JMI ADVISORY SERVICES LIMITED
Address:	85–87 Jermyn Street, London SW1Y 6JD
Telephone:	01–930 7107
Telex:	917137 ERIG
Fax:	01–930 7100

Company Details

Full-time Executives:	2
Type of Organisation:	Independent
Funds Managed:	JMI Seed Capital Limited
Total Capital Invested:	£288,000
Total Capital Available:	£1,050,000
Specialisations:	Information technology, Communications, Health Care
Current Portfolio Size:	6
Investments as	
Lead Investor:	Genetic Testing Ltd, Stewkie Systems Ltd

Investment Preferences

Minimum Investment:	£5,000
Preferred Investment:	£75–£100,000
Type of Funding:	Equity only
Stage of Investment:	Seed capital
Investment Conditions:	Substantial growth potential
Industry Preferences:	Advanced technology
Geographical Preferences:	2 hours travel from London

Contacts:	Sy Joffe, Richard Poulden

Company:	JOHNSTON DEVELOPMENT CAPITAL LTD
Address:	Johnston House, Hatchlands Road, Redhill, Surrey RH1 1BG
Telephone:	0737 242466
Telex:	27641
Fax:	0737 221082

Company Details

Full-time Executives:	3
Type of Organisation:	Subsidiary of Johnston Group PLC (a quoted engineering group)

Funds Managed:	—
Total Capital Invested:	£350,000
Total Capital Available:	£1,150,000 (likely to be extended)
Specialisations:	General
Current Portfolio Size:	1
Investment as Lead Investor:	—

Investment Preferences

Minimum Investment:	£100,000
Preferred Investment:	£250,000
Type of Funding:	Equity preferred, loans/prefs possible
Stage of Investment:	Start-up/Expansion/Buy-out
Investment Conditions:	High potential growth. Director involvement required
Industry Preferences:	None
Geographical Preferences:	UK only

Contacts:	Nicholas Panes, David Currie, Sean MacDonald

Company:	**KENT INVESTMENTS LTD**
Address:	Brenchley House, Week Street, Maidstone, Kent ME14 1RF
Telephone:	0622 679976
Telex:	965212 KENLIB
Fax:	0622 687351

Company Details

Full-time Executives:	2
Type of Organisation:	Subsidiary of Kent Economic Development Board
Funds Managed:	—
Total Capital Invested:	£800,000
Total Capital Available:	£700,000
Specialisations:	—
Current Portfolio Size:	14
Investments as Lead Investor:	—

Investment Preferences

Minimum Investment:	£20,000
Preferred Investment:	£30,000–£100,000

Type of Funding:	Equity
Stage of Investment:	—
Investment Conditions:	—
Industry Preferences:	All except Retail, Agriculture & Transport
Geographical Preferences:	Kent based or moving to Kent.

| Contacts: | David Morse, Colin Saunders |

Company:	**KLEINWORT BENSON DEVELOPMENT CAPITAL LIMITED**
Address:	20 Fenchurch Street, London EC3P 3DB
Telephone:	01–623 8000
Telex:	888531
Fax:	01–626 8616

Company Details

Full-time Executives:	7
Type of Organisation:	Merchant bank subsidiary
Funds Managed:	Kleinwort Development Fund
Total Capital Invested:	£70m
Total Capital Available:	No limit
Specialisations:	None
Current Portfolio Size:	65
Investments as Lead Investor:	Istel Ltd; JMH; Regency Life; Stewart McColl Associates; U.A.P.T; Commslogic; Reuter Simkin

Investment Preferences

Minimum Investment:	£300,000
Preferred Investment:	£1m–£2m
Type of Funding:	Equity only and equity with loan
Stage of Investment:	All considered but seed capital unlikely
Investment Conditions:	Realisable in 4–7 years
Industry Preferences:	None
Geographical Preferences:	UK & Europe

| Contacts: | B.M. (Barry) Dean, E.T. (Emyr) Hughes, Miss J.M. (Joanna) James, Mrs S. (Sarah) Moberley, Mr A. (Andy) Pomfret, Mr R. (Richard) Green, Mr I. (Ian) Grant |

Company:	**KORDA & COMPANY LIMITED**
Address:	5th Floor, 18–20 Farringdon Lane, London EC1R 3AU
Telephone:	01–253 5882
Telex:	94018597 KORDA G
Fax:	01–251 4837

Company Details

Full-time Executives:	7
Type of Organisation:	Independent
Funds Managed:	The Korda Seed Capital Fund Limited Partnership
Total Capital Invested:	£400,000
Total Capital Available:	£5m
Specialisations:	Information Technology, Life Sciences and New Materials
Current Portfolio Size:	6
Investments as Lead Investor:	Xenova Ltd; Archaeus Ltd; Satellite Media Services Ltd

Investment Preferences

Minimum Investment:	None
Preferred Investment:	£50,000–£400,000
Type of Funding:	Equity and Loan
Stage of Investment:	Seed and start-up
Investment Conditions:	—
Industry Preferences:	Technology
Geographical Preferences:	UK and Continental Europe
Contacts:	Pierre de Vries, Tazewell Wilson, Keith Mallinson, Vida Finnis

Company:	**LANCASHIRE ENTERPRISES LIMITED**
Address:	Enterprise House, 17 Ribblesdale Place, Winckley Square, Preston PR1 3NA
Telephone:	0772 203020
Telex:	67343 LANENT G
Fax:	0772 204129

Company Details

Full-time Executives:	7
Type of Organisation:	Subsidiary of Lancashire Enterprises Ltd
Funds Managed:	—
Total Capital Invested:	£7m
Total Capital Available:	£10m
Specialisations:	—
Current Portfolio Size:	45
Investments as Lead Investor:	—

Investment Preferences

Minimum Investment:	£50,000
Preferred Investment:	£100,000–£300,000
Type of Funding:	Equity/Preference Share Capital/Loan Capital
Stage of Investment:	All stages considered
Investment Conditions:	—
Industry Preferences:	All sectors considered
Geographical Preferences:	North West of England

Contacts:	Richard Bamford, Robert Sheffrin, David Hall

Company:	**LARPENT NEWTON & CO LTD**
Address:	4th Floor, 24/26 Baltic Street, London EC1Y 0TB
Telephone:	01–251 9111
Telex:	94011991 LNCO G
Fax:	01–251 2609

Company Details

Full-time Executives:	6
Type of Organisation:	Independent
Funds Managed:	The Growth Fund Ltd
Total Capital Invested:	£5m
Total Capital Available:	New £10m fund due to be launched
Specialisations:	None
Current Portfolio Size:	12
Investments as Lead Investor:	BioTal Ltd, Delta Communications plc

Investment Preferences

Minimum Investment:	None
Preferred Investment:	£200,000–£1m
Type of Funding:	Equity only and equity with loan
Stage of Investment:	Start-up, expansion and buy-out
Investment Conditions:	Profit potential of at least £800,000 in 5–7 years
Industry Preferences:	None
Geographical Preferences:	UK based

Contact:	Charles Breese

Company:	**LEGAL & GENERAL VENTURES LTD**
Address:	Bucklersbury House, 3 Queen Victoria Street, London EC4N 8EL
Telephone:	01–489 1888
Telex:	892971
Fax:	01–489 9066

Company Details

Full-time Executives:	6
Type of Organisation:	Independent
Funds Managed:	Legal & General Venture & Development Capital Fund
Total Capital Invested:	£120m
Total Capital Available:	£20m p.a. +
Specialisations:	None
Current Portfolio Size:	140
Investments as Lead Investor:	—

Investment Preferences

Minimum Investment:	£250,000
Preferred Investment:	£500,000–£1,000,000
Type of Funding:	Equity and equity with loan
Stage of Investment:	Expansion/MBO/MBI
Investment Conditions:	Up to 20% equity stake. Agreed exit strategy
Industry Preferences:	None
Geographical Preferences:	UK

Contacts:	Charles Peal, Eric Cooper, Adrian Johnson, Peter Laszlo, Ian Taylor, Jenny Fenton, Bernard Jenkin, John Jervoise, Ian Wilson

Company:	LICA DEVELOPMENT CAPITAL LIMITED
Address:	102 Jermyn Street, London SW1Y 6EE
Telephone:	01–839 7707
Telex:	—
Fax:	01–839 7707/01–839 4363

Company Details

Full-time Executives:	8
Type of Organisation:	Independent
Funds Managed:	SELECT Industries Trust
Total Capital Invested:	£2m
Total Capital Available:	£25m
Specialisations:	Biosciences, meditech, distribution, manufacturing, micro-chip/digital applications, etc
Current Portfolio Size:	5
Investments as Lead Investor:	Bioseparation Associates; Emeritus Corp; Intercim Corp; Reece plc; Tower Bridge Holdings

Investment Preferences

Minimum Investment:	£100,000
Preferred Investment:	£500,000–£1,500,000
Type of Funding:	Equity (and loan placing)
Stage of Investment:	Start-up/expansion/MBI/recovery
Investment Conditions:	Sound management team is essential
Industry Preferences:	High growth potential in both leading and basic industries
Geographical Preferences:	EC and US

Contacts:	Stephen Hill, Mary McGahan, Franco Racca, Vanessa Waddell, Mark Wordsworth

Company:	LLOYDS DEVELOPMENT CAPITAL LTD
Address:	40–66 Queen Victoria Street, London EC4P 4EL
Telephone:	01–248 4275/01–236 4940
	Birmingham 021–200 1787
	Leeds 0532 441001

Telex:	—
Fax:	01–329 4900/Birmingham 021–236 5269
	Leeds 0532 421822

Company Details

Full-time Executives:	13 in London, 3 in Birmingham, 3 in Leeds
Type of Organisation:	Captive
Funds Managed:	Lloyds Development Capital
Total Capital Invested:	£40m
Total Capital Available:	Unlimited
Specialisations:	None
Current Portfolio Size:	75
Investments as	
Lead Investor:	Evans Healthcare; Encon Insulation Services; Leaquester Plc; JBA International Plc; VSEL (co-led with Lloyds Merchant Bank)

Investment Preferences

Minimum Investment:	£200,000
Preferred Investment:	£500,000–£2m
Type of Funding:	Equity only and Equity with loan
Stage of Investment:	Expansion/Buy-out
Investment Conditions:	Well-managed companies with growth potential. Pre-tax profits in excess of £100,000
Industry Preferences:	None
Geographical Preferences:	UK only

Contacts:	R. Hollidge (Managing Director), T.J.U. Inglefield (Deputy Managing Director), I.T. Burns (Director), K.G. Carpenter (Director), R.J. Ashmead (Director).
	Birmingham: M.W. Joseph (Director)
	Leeds: G.J. Weaver (Director)

Company:	**LONDON WALL INVESTMENTS**
Address:	25 Copthall Avenue, London EC2R 7DR
Telephone:	01–638 5362
Telex:	297451
Fax:	01–374 0263

Company Details

Full-time Executives:	4
Type of Organisation:	Investment Department of Merchant Bank
Funds Managed:	Various investment trusts and pension fund clients
Total Capital Invested:	£60m
Total Capital Available:	Open
Specialisations:	General
Current Portfolio Size:	39
Investments as Lead Investor:	—

Investment Preferences

Minimum Investment:	£500,000
Preferred Investment:	£1,000,000
Type of Funding:	Equity & Loan
Stage of Investment:	Expansion, MBO, MBI
Investment Conditions:	None
Industry Preferences:	None
Geographical Preferences:	None

Contacts:	Martin Pritchard, Jan Sawkins, William Crewdson, Andrew Benns

Company:	**MARCH INVESTMENT FUND LTD**
Address:	36–39 Waterfront Quay, Salford Quays, Manchester M5 2XW
Telephone:	061–872 3676
Telex:	669225
Fax:	061–848 0181

Company Details

Full-time Executives:	4
Type of Organisation:	Independent (collaborative Venture March Consulting Group/British Gas Pension Funds)
Funds Managed:	March Investment Fund, MCRB Scheme
Total Capital Invested:	£12m
Total Capital Available:	£25m (£4m p.a.)
Specialisations:	Manufacturing industry, energy, marketing, recruitment et al
Current Portfolio Size:	13

Investments as
   Lead Investor: Berk Ltd; Bulldog Tools Ltd; James North Foot-wear Ltd; Stoodley Holdings Ltd

Investment Preferences

Minimum Investment:	£250,000
Preferred Investment:	£600,000–£1.5m
Type of Funding:	Flexible but always with Equity
Stage of Investment:	Expansion, Buy-out, sometimes start-up
Investment Conditions:	Preference given to buy-out or expansions of existing profitable businesses
Industry Preferences:	'Traditional' manufacturing industries or the service sector
Geographical Preferences:	UK, especially North West and Midlands

Contacts:	Richard S. Marshall, William J. Hopkins

Company:	**MERCURY ASSET MANAGEMENT**
Address:	33 King William Street, London EC4R 9AS
Telephone:	01–280 2800
Telex:	8953927 WIMLON G
Fax:	01–280 2810/2820/2830

Company Details

Full-time Executives:	4
Type of Organisation:	Independent
Funds Managed:	Mercury Unquoted Securities Trust
	Various Pension Funds
Total Capital Invested:	£100m
Total Capital Available:	Unlimited
Specialisations:	None
Current Portfolio Size:	70

Investments as
   Lead Investor: Allied Steel & Wire; Kentish Times Newspapers; York Trailer Holdings; Argus Press

Investment Preferences

Minimum Investment:	£500,000
Preferred Investment:	£2m
Type of Funding:	Equity/Mezzanine
Stage of Investment:	Expansion, MBO/MBI

Investment Conditions:	Potential for realisation of investment through sale or flotation within seven years
Industry Preferences:	None
Geographical Preferences:	None

Contacts:	Roger Llewellyn, Sandra O'Neill, Frances Jacob, Ian Armitage

Company:	**MERSEYSIDE ENTERPRISE BOARD LTD**
Address:	Third Floor, Royal Liver Building, Water St, Liverpool L3 1HT
Telephone:	051–236 0221
Telex:	—
Fax:	051–236 3666

Company Details

Full-time Executives:	4
Type of Organisation:	Independent
Funds Managed:	CLM Unit Trust
	Merseyside Enterprise Board Main Fund
	Wirral Investments for Supporting Enterprises
	The Merseyside Small Firms Fund Ltd
Total Capital Invested:	£5m
Total Capital Available:	£5.6m
Specialisations:	None
Current Portfolio Size:	52
Investments as	
Lead Investor:	Freshfield Foods Ltd, Powell of Schofield Ltd, Tuf Loc Ltd

Investment Preferences

Minimum Investment:	£10,000
Preferred Investment:	£100,000–£200,000
Type of Funding:	Equity and loan
Stage of Investment:	—
Investment Conditions:	—
Industry Preferences:	—
Geographical Preferences:	North-West England

Contacts:	K. Abbott, P. Morton

Company:	MIDLAND MONTAGU VENTURES LIMITED
Address:	10 Lower Thames Street, London EC3R 6AE
Telephone:	01–260 9911
Telex:	887213
Fax:	01–220 7265

Company Details

Full-time Executives:	14
Type of Organisation:	Captive
Funds Managed:	In addition to own funds MMV manages Moracrest Investments Limited
Total Capital Invested:	£150m
Total Capital Available:	Unlimited
Specialisations:	General management expertise in many industries
Current Portfolio Size:	135
Investments as	
Lead Investor:	Amari; GBE International; Porth Decorative Products; Lewis's Department Stores; SIBEC

Investment Preferences

Minimum Investment:	£500,000
Preferred Investment:	£1.5m +
Type of Funding:	Primarily equity, but loan finance considered as part of an equity package
Stage of Investment:	Mostly Management Buy-Outs, Buy-Ins, Share Purchases and Expansion
Investment Conditions:	Strong Management, growth prospects
Industry Preferences:	None
Geographical Preferences:	UK, Western Europe, USA, Australia

Contacts:	Ian Taylor, John Brandon, David Casstles and Dennis Freedman

Company:	MIM DEVELOPMENT CAPITAL LIMITED
Address:	11 Devonshire Square, London EC2M 4YR
Telephone:	01–626 3434
Telex:	886108
Fax:	01–623 3339

Company Details

Full-time Executives:	5
Type of Organisation:	Venture and development capital subsidiary of MIM Britannia Fund Management Group
Funds Managed:	Major quoted investment trusts, local authority pension funds and own development capital fund
Total Capital Invested:	£90m
Total Capital Available:	Open
Specialisations:	No specialisation
Current Portfolio Size:	135
Investments as	
Lead Investor:	Alma Caledonia Limited; Diamond Group Holdings PLC; Scottish Highland Hotels Limited

Investment Preferences

Minimum Investment:	£250,000
Preferred Investment:	£250,000–£3m
Type of Funding:	Equity packages
Stage of Investment:	Expansion and Buy-out
Investment Conditions:	No fixed conditions
Industry Preferences:	Any
Geographical Preferences:	UK

Contacts:	Richard Connell, Alexander Reid, Brian Phillips

Company:	**MTI MANAGERS LIMITED**
Address:	70 St Albans Road, Watford, Herts WD1 1RP
Telephone:	(0923) 50244
Telex:	—
Fax:	(0923) 247783

Company Details

Full-time Executives:	7
Type of Organisation:	Independent
Funds Managed:	Managed Technology Investors
Total Capital Invested:	£6.25m
Total Capital Available:	£9.1m
Specialisations:	Electronics, hardware, software, materials, automation, biotechnology
Current Portfolio Size:	12

Investments as
  Lead Investor: Fixit (Adhesive); Prism Electronics; BritCair; Pace
                     Communications; Linx Printing Technologies

Investment Preferences

Minimum Investment: £200,000
Preferred Investment: £250,000–£750,000
Type of Funding: Equity
Stage of Investment: Start-up, Expansion, Buy-out, Rescue
Investment Conditions: None
Industry Preferences: High technology, product companies
Geographical Preferences: UK only

Contacts: Dr Paul Castle, Richard Ford

Company: **MURRAY JOHNSTONE LIMITED**
Address: 7 West Nile Street, Glasgow G1 2PX
Telephone: 041–226 3131
Telex: 778667
Fax: 041–248 5420

Company Details

Full-time Executives: 13
Type of Organisation: Independent
Funds Managed: Murray Electronics plc
                           Murray Technology Investments plc
                           Murray Ventures plc
                           Murray Johnstone LBO Fund LP
                           Murraystone Investments Ltd
Total Capital Invested: £100m +
Total Capital Available: £100m +
Specialisations: None
Current Portfolio Size: 100 +
Investments as
  Lead Investor: Caithness Glass; Clairmont; Ritchie Print Pack;
                           Strathgordon; Paisley Hyer

Investment Preferences

Minimum Investment: £100,000
Preferred Investment: £250,000–£10m
Type of Funding: Equity with loan

Stage of Investment:	Acquisition and expansion, MBO/MBI
Investment Conditions:	Management, product and markets
Industry Preferences:	None
Geographical Preferences:	UK, Europe and USA

Contacts:	Ross Peters, Iain Tulloch, David MacLellan, Geoff Burns

Company:	**MYNSHUL VENTURES LIMITED**
Address:	Cheshire House, 18–20 Booth Street, Manchester M2 4AN
Telephone:	061–236 1334
Telex:	—
Fax:	061–228 6355

Company Details

Full-time Executives:	3
Type of Organisation:	Independent
Funds Managed:	None
Total Capital Invested:	£2.5m
Total Capital Available:	£10m
Specialisations:	—
Current Portfolio Size:	12
Investments as Lead Investor:	—

Investment Preferences

Minimum Investment:	£50,000
Preferred Investment:	£200,000
Type of Funding:	Loan/Equity Capital
Stage of Investment:	—
Investment Conditions:	—
Industry Preferences:	Manufacturing & Service Industry
Geographical Preferences:	North Midlands & North of England

Contacts:	Iain Campbell, Peter Champlin, Kevin Davies

Company:	**N. M. ROTHSCHILD ASSET MANAGEMENT LIMITED**
Address:	Five Arrows House, St Swithin's Lane, London EC4N 8NR
Telephone:	01–280 5000

Telex:	888031
Fax:	01–634 2885

Company Details

Full-time Executives:	6
Type of Organisation:	Independent
Funds Managed:	Advisers to Biotechnology Investments Limited
Total Capital Invested:	$105m
Total Capital Available:	$35m
Specialisations:	Biotechnology and Medical Technology
Current Portfolio Size:	58 (quoted: 30; unquoted: 28)
Investments as	
Lead Investor:	British Biotechnology Ltd; Gensia Pharmaceuticals Inc; Immunetech Pharmaceuticals Inc

Investment Preferences

Minimum Investment:	$0.5m
Preferred Investment:	$1.0m–2.0m
Type of Funding:	Equity
Stage of Investment:	Any – preference early stage
Investment Conditions:	None
Industry Preferences:	Biotechnology and medical technology exclusively
Geographical Preferences:	None

Contacts:	Jeremy Curnock Cook, Susan Flynn

Company:	**NATIONAL WESTMINSTER GROWTH OPTIONS LIMITED**
Address:	King's Cross House, 200 Pentonville Road, London N1 9LH
Telephone:	01–239 8563
Telex:	—
Fax:	01–239 8900

Company Details

Full-time Executives:	6
Type of Organisation:	Subsidiary of National Westminster Bank PLC
Funds Managed:	N/A
Total Capital Invested:	£5m
Total Capital Available:	Unlimited
Specialisations:	—

Current Portfolio Size:	52
Investments as	
Lead Investor:	Not disclosed

Investment Preferences

Minimum Investment:	£25,000
Preferred Investment:	Maximum £300,000 (plus conventional banking facilities)
Type of Funding:	Equity and Loan
Stage of Investment:	All considered except seedcorn
Investment Conditions:	Flexible
Industry Preferences:	—
Geographical Preferences:	UK based

Contacts:	John Jeffries (Ext. 8599)
	Alan Hinton (Ext. 8598)
	Ian Andrews (Ext. 3089)
	Chris Cook (Ext. 3088)

Company:	NEWMARKET VENTURE CAPITAL PLC
Address:	14–20 Chiswell Street, London EC1Y 4TY
Telephone:	01–638 2521
Telex:	934084 NEWVC G
Fax:	01–638 8409

Company Details

Full-time Executives:	3
Type of Organisation:	Independent
Funds Managed:	N/A
Total Capital Invested:	£45m
Total Capital Available:	£2.7m
Specialisations:	Mainly electronics and bio-sciences
Current Portfolio Size:	77
Investments as	
Lead Investor:	UMI; Cell Systems; Prosys; Synoptics

Investment Preferences

Minimum Investment:	£250,000
Preferred Investment:	£250,000–£1m
Type of Funding:	Mostly equity, some loan

Stage of Investment:	Start-up/Early Stage, Expansion
Investment Conditions:	Sound business plan which supports ultimate sales and profits
Industry Preferences:	Companies developing new innovative technologies
Geographical Preferences:	UK & USA

Contacts:	Alan Henderson, Caroline Vaughan, Tom Shaw

Company:	**NORTH OF ENGLAND VENTURES LTD**
Address:	Cheshire House, 18–20 Booth Street, Manchester M2 4AN
Telephone:	061–236 6600
Telex:	—
Fax:	01–236 6650

Company Details

Full-time Executives:	3
Type of Organisation:	Joint venture with Schroder Ventures and Rickitt Mitchell & Partners
Funds Managed:	North of England Venture Fund
Total Capital Invested:	—
Total Capital Available:	£19m
Specialisations:	None
Current Portfolio Size:	—
Investments as Lead Investor:	—

Investment Preferences

Minimum Investment:	£200,000
Preferred Investment:	£200,000–£2m
Type of Funding:	Equity with loan
Stage of Investment:	Start-up; Expansion; MBO; MBI; Replacement
Investment Conditions:	Open
Industry Preferences:	Not Property
Geographical Preferences:	Midlands and North of England

Contacts:	Peter J. Folkman, Kelvyn G. Derrick, Michael D. Gabriel

Company:	NORTHERN VENTURE MANAGERS LIMITED
Address:	Centro House, 3 Cloth Market, Newcastle upon Tyne NE1 1EE
Telephone:	(091) 232 7068
Telex:	—
Fax:	(091) 232 4070

Company Details

Full-time Executives:	5
Type of Organisation:	Independent
Funds Managed:	Northern Investors
Total Capital Invested:	£4.9m
Total Capital Available:	£1.6m
Specialisations:	None
Current Portfolio Size:	25
Investments as	
Lead Investor:	Pentagon Chemicals Limited; R. Norman Limited; Northumbria Biologicals Limited; Wilson Walton Group Limited

Investment Preferences

Minimum Investment:	£25,000
Preferred Investment:	£200,000–£400,000
Type of Funding:	Flexible but always with equity participation
Stage of Investment:	All stages
Investment Conditions:	None specified
Industry Preferences:	None
Geographical Preferences:	North/Scotland

Contacts:	Michael Denny, Tim Levett, Roland Tate

Company:	NORWICH UNION VENTURE CAPITAL LTD
Address:	PO Box No 53, Surrey Street, Norwich NR1 3TE
Telephone:	0603 683803
Telex:	97388 NUHO G
Fax:	0603 681120

Company Details

Full-time Executives:	4

Type of Organisation:	Venture Capital Subsidiary of Norwich Union Life Insurance Society
Funds Managed:	Own Fund
Total Capital Invested:	£26.4m
Total Capital Available:	£5.7m (further tranches available as applied for)
Specialisations:	None
Current Portfolio Size:	53
Investments as	
Lead Investor:	Crown Crest Enterprises Ltd

Investment Preferences

Minimum Investment:	£100,000
Preferred Investment:	£100,000 to £1m
Type of Funding:	Normally Equity only but will consider loan as part of a package
Stage of Investment:	Preference for development or management buy-out finance but will consider well researched start-ups
Investment Conditions:	UK registered unquoted companies demonstrating major growth potential
Industry Preferences:	All sectors considered except property development and financial services
Geographical Preferences:	UK

Contact:	Geoff Evans

Company:	**OAKLAND INVESTMENT MANAGEMENT LTD**
Address:	Ramsbury House, High Street, Hungerford, Berkshire RG17 0LY
Telephone:	0488 83555
Telex:	848130
Fax:	0488 84924

Company Details

Full-time Executives:	7
Type of Organisation:	Independent
Funds Managed:	Oakland Development Capital Fund
	Thames Valley Ventures
	Alpha Business Expansion Funds
	Oakland Business Expansion Fund

Total Capital Invested:	£17m
Total Capital Available:	£20m
Specialisations:	Engineering, General Manufacturing, Leisure, Fashion, Multiple Retail, Distribution, Consumer Products
Current Portfolio Size:	50 +
Investments as	
Lead Investor:	Gor-Ray Ltd; Elegant Ways PLC; Waterslides Plc; Sinks & Things Ltd.

Investment Preferences

Minimum Investment:	£400,000
Preferred Investment:	£1m +
Type of Funding:	Flexible, mostly equity
Stage of Investment:	All stages but emphasis on expansion
Investment Conditions:	Strong growth potential
Industry Preferences:	See specialisations but others considered
Geographical Preferences:	Southern half of UK

Contacts:	Ron Fidler, Gordon Kenneth, Philip Margesson

Company:	**OCTAGON INVESTMENT MANAGEMENT LIMITED**
Address:	Cambridge Science Park, Milton Road, Cambridge CB4 4WE
Telephone:	0223 863033
Telex:	—
Fax:	0223 862941

Company Details

Full-time Executives:	2
Type of Organisation:	Independent
Funds Managed:	Hoare Octagon BES Funds
	Octagon BES Funds
	The Euroventures UK & Ireland Programme
Total Capital Invested:	£8m
Total Capital Available:	£5.8m
Specialisations:	None
Current Portfolio Size:	28

Investments as	
Lead Investor:	Percom Ltd; CAL Videographics Ltd; Robot (UK) Ltd; Integrated Information Technology Ltd

Investment Preferences

Minimum Investment:	£100,000
Preferred Investment:	£100,000–£500,000
Type of Funding:	Primarily Equity
Stage of Investment:	Start-up and expansion capital
Investment Conditions:	Strong growth potential
Industry Preferences:	Information industries – computing, telecommunications, broadcasting, advertising
Geographical Preferences:	UK & Ireland, Continental Europe

Contacts:	Chris Rowlands, Ian Barton

Company:	**OXFORD SEEDCORN CAPITAL LIMITED**
Address:	213 Woodstock Road, Oxford OX2 7AD
Telephone:	0865 53535
Telex:	—
Fax:	0865 512976

Company Details

Full-time Executives:	3
Type of Organisation:	Independent
Funds Managed:	Oxford Seedcorn Capital
	Oxford Seed Capital Fund
Total Capital Invested:	£368,000
Total Capital Available:	£1,175,000
Specialisations:	Engineering, Medical, Technology.
Current Portfolio Size:	8
Investments as	
Lead Investor:	Sophos Ltd; Auric International Ltd

Investment Preferences

Minimum Investment:	£10,000
Preferred Investment:	£50,000
Type of Funding:	Equity and Equity related
Stage of Investment:	Seed, start-up and early stage development
Investment Conditions:	Niche markets with large growth potential
Industry Preferences:	Mainly Technology

Geographical Preferences:	Within easy reach of Oxford
Contacts:	Antony Costley-White, John Laurie, Jonathan Welfare

Company:	PHILDREW VENTURES
Address:	Triton Court, 14 Finsbury Square, London EC2A 1PD
Telephone:	01–628 6366
Telex:	268934
Fax:	01–638 2817

Company Details

Full-time Executives:	8
Type of Organisation:	Independent
Funds Managed:	The Phildrew Ventures Fund; The Phillips & Drew Development Capital Fund
Total Capital Invested:	£65m
Total Capital Available:	£138m
Specialisations:	Retail, Consumer goods, Industrial, Financial Services
Current Portfolio Size:	45
Investments as Lead Investor:	Square Grip; Admiral Homes; UCI Group; Norwich Corrugated

Investment Preferences

Minimum Investment:	£0.5m
Preferred Investment:	£1m +
Type of Funding:	Equity packages
Stage of Investment:	Buy-outs, Buy-ins and Expansion Capital
Investment Conditions:	Preferably £5m + capitalisations
Industry Preferences:	None
Geographical Preferences:	UK & Europe

Contacts:	Charles Gonszor, Tim Hart, Ian Hawkins, Ron Hobbs, Robert Jenkins, Frank Neale

Company:	PINE STREET INVESTMENTS LTD
Address:	Bowater House West, 68 Knightsbridge, London SW1X 7LT

Telephone:	01–225 3911
Telex:	—
Fax:	01–581 0131

Company Details

Full-time Executives:	7
Type of Organisation:	Independent
Funds Managed:	Investment Partnership
Total Capital Invested:	£7.5m
Total Capital Available:	£50m
Specialisations:	—
Current Portfolio Size:	10
Investments as	
Lead Investor:	—

Investment Preferences

Minimum Investment:	£250,000
Preferred Investment:	£1m +
Type of Funding:	Equity/Loan Capital
Stage of Investment:	Venture/Development
Investment Conditions:	—
Industry Preferences:	Financial Service
Geographical Preferences:	UK & Europe

Contacts:	R.A. Berman, N.J. Webber

Company:	**PIPER INVESTMENT MANAGEMENT LTD**
Address:	Eardley House, 182–184 Campden Hill Road, London W8 7AS
Telephone:	01–727 3866
Telex:	—
Fax:	01–727 8969

Company Details

Full-time Executives:	2
Type of Organisation:	Independent
Funds Managed:	The Piper Retail Fund
Total Capital Invested:	£2m
Total Capital Available:	£5m
Specialisations:	Retail and Leisure only
Current Portfolio Size:	6

Investments as
  Lead Investor: —

Investment Preferences

Minimum Investment:	£100,000
Preferred Investment:	£250,000–£750,000
Type of Funding:	Equity packages
Stage of Investment:	All stages
Investment Conditions:	None
Industry Preferences:	Retail and Leisure
Geographical Preferences:	UK

Contacts: Christopher Curry, Crispin Tweddell

Company:	**PRELUDE TECHNOLOGY INVESTMENTS LIMITED**
Address:	280 Science Park, Milton Road, Cambridge CB4 4WE
Telephone:	(0223) 423132
Telex:	—
Fax:	(0223) 420869

Company Details

Full-time Executives:	4
Type of Organisation:	Independent
Funds Managed:	Prelude Technology Fund
Total Capital Invested:	£3.3m
Total Capital Available:	£1.9m (Additional funds being raised)
Specialisations:	Technology based
Current Portfolio Size:	10
Investments as Lead Investor:	Elmjet Limited

Investment Preferences

Minimum Investment:	£10,000 (Seed Investment)
Preferred Investment:	£250,000–£500,000
Type of Funding:	Equity plus related loan/preference shares
Stage of Investment:	Seed Capital/Start-up and early expansion
Investment Conditions:	Niche markets with substantial growth potential
Industry Preferences:	New technology

Geographical Preferences:	UK based businesses accessible from Cambridge
Contacts:	Robert Hook, Keith Padbury, Stephen Jones

Company:	**PRUDENTIAL VENTURE MANAGERS LIMITED**
Address:	Audrey House, Ely Place, London EC1N 6SN
Telephone:	01–831 7747
Telex:	264504
Fax:	01–831 9528

Company Details

Full-time Executives:	12
Type of Organisation:	The venture and development capital arm of Prudential Corporation plc
Funds Managed:	—
Total Capital Invested:	£200m
Total Capital Available:	Open
Specialisations:	Management Buy-outs and underwriting the larger MBOs in all sectors
Current Portfolio Size:	185
Investments as	
Lead Investor:	Allders Ltd; Westbury Homes Ltd; Gomme Limited; St Regis Holdings Ltd; Sunday Correspondent; Harpur Holdings Ltd

Investment Preferences

Minimum Investment:	£500,000
Preferred Investment:	£500,000–£20m
Type of Funding:	Equity and equity related funding
Stage of Investment:	All stages
Investment Conditions:	Companies with above average growth potential
Industry Preferences:	Any
Geographical Preferences:	UK, Europe, USA

Contacts:	Paul Brooks, Michael Geary, Martin Clarke, Jonathan Morgan, Gus Guest, Carol Kennedy, Nigel McConnell, Lindsay Stuart, Marcus Thompson, Andrew Smith

Company:	QUAYLE MUNRO LIMITED
Address:	42 Charlotte Square, Edinburgh EH2 4HQ
Telephone:	031–226 4421
Telex:	72244
Fax:	031–225 3391

Company Details

Full-time Executives:	6
Type of Organisation:	Private company managing institutionally backed, independent funds
Funds Managed:	East of Scotland Industrial Investments PLC
Total Capital Invested:	£15m
Total Capital Available:	£19m
Specialisations:	None
Current Portfolio Size:	21
Investments as Lead Investor:	Shanks & McEwan Group plc; EPS (Moulders) Limited; International Twist Drill (Holdings) Limited; Whelmar Homes Limited

Investment Preferences

Minimum Investment:	£250,000
Preferred Investment:	Up to £1m
Type of Funding:	Equity and/or Loan Capital
Stage of Investment:	Expansion, buy-outs and buy-ins
Investment Conditions:	Well established
Industry Preferences:	None
Geographical Preferences:	Mainly UK

Contacts:	Ian Q. Jones, D. Michael Munro, Robert W.L. Legget, G.R. St. C. Harden

Company:	ROTHSCHILD VENTURES LIMITED
Address:	New Court, St Swithin's Lane, London EC4P 4DU
Telephone:	01–280 5000
Telex:	888031
Fax:	01–929 1643

Company Details

Full-time Executives:	6
Type of Organisation:	Captive
Funds Managed:	New Court Ventures
	Old Court Ventures
	Various Pension fund clients
Total Capital Invested:	£21m
Total Capital Available:	Open
Specialisations:	All industries considered
Current Portfolio Size:	47
Investments as	
Lead Investor:	F.I. Group; Headline Book Publishing; Mentor Systems; Pickwick Group; Virago Press

Investment Preferences

Minimum Investment:	£100,000
Preferred Investment:	Up to £2.5m
Type of Funding:	Equity related
Stage of Investment:	Start-up, Expansion, Management Buy-out, Management Buy-in, Secondary Share Purchase, Turnaround
Investment Conditions:	None
Industry Preferences:	None
Geographical Preferences:	Throughout UK and Europe

Contacts:	Jeremy Dawson, Nigel Street, Nicholas Mac Nay, Benedict Kelly, James Stewart, Alex Smith

Company:	**SCHRODER VENTURES**
Address:	20 Southampton Street, London WC2E 7QG
Telephone:	01–379 5010
Telex:	—
Fax:	01–240 5072

Company Details

Full-time Executives:	16
Type of Organisation:	Independent partnership
Funds Managed:	Schroder UK Venture Funds I & II
	Schroder UK Buy-Out Fund

Total Capital Invested:	£96m
Total Capital Available:	£180m
Specialisations:	Electronics, Consumer, Medical
Current Portfolio Size:	50
Investments as Lead Investor:	Parker; Xenova; Merryweathers; Haleworth; Glass Glover

Investment Preferences

Minimum Investment:	£500,000
Preferred Investment:	None
Type of Funding:	Equity with loan
Stage of Investment:	Start-up, Expansion, Buy-out
Investment Conditions:	None
Industry Preferences:	Not property
Geographical Preferences:	UK

| Contact: | Jon Moulton |

Company:	SCIMITAR DEVELOPMENT CAPITAL LIMITED
Address:	Osprey House, 78 Wigmore Street, London W1H 9DQ
Telephone:	01–487 5914
Telex:	269762
Fax:	01–487 5048

Company Details

Full-time Executives:	3
Type of Organisation:	Company owned by Standard Chartered Merchant Bank & Executive Directors
Funds Managed:	Scimitar Development Capital Fund
	Scimitar Development Capital 'B' Fund
Total Capital Invested:	US$15m
Total Capital Available:	US$42m
Specialisations:	General
Current Portfolio Size:	9
Investments as Lead Investor:	Speeflo Manufacturing Corp; Pietro's Pizza Corp; International Twist Drill Ltd; The Movie Exchange Inc.

Investment Preferences

Minimum Investment:	£300,000
Preferred Investment:	£750,000–£2m
Type of Funding:	Equity or Equity related
Stage of Investment:	Expansion, Buy-outs, Buy-ins, Acquisitions
Investment Conditions:	Good management, profitable potential for growth and listing
Industry Preferences:	None
Geographical Preferences:	UK or USA

Contacts:	Richard Arthur, Peter Dale, Dennis Hallahane

Company:	SCOTTISH DEVELOPMENT AGENCY
Address:	120 Bothwell Street, Glasgow G2 7JP
Telephone:	041–248 2700
Telex:	777600
Fax:	041–221 3217

Company Details

Full-time Executives:	10
Type of Organisation:	Government sponsored
Funds Managed:	—
Total Capital Invested:	£30m
Total Capital Available:	Open
Specialisations:	General
Current Portfolio Size:	145
Investments as Lead Investor:	Stoddard Holdings plc

Investment Preferences

Minimum Investment:	£10,000
Preferred Investment:	£200,000–£1m
Type of Funding:	Equity, Loans, Royalties and Guarantees
Stage of Investment:	Pre Start-up only rarely. All other stages of funding available
Investment Conditions:	Committed management team which can exploit niche market opportunities. Commercial rate of return

Industry Preferences:	Priority areas are healthcare/electronics, energy related, service industries and advanced engineering. However, investments are undertaken in all other sectors
Geographical Preferences:	Scotland

Contacts:	Donald Patience, Director Investment; Frank Gow, Investment Manager; Douglas Kearney, Investment Manager; Bill Logie, Investment Manager

Company:	SECURITY PACIFIC HOARE GOVETT EQUITY VENTURES LIMITED
Address:	4 Broadgate, London EC2M 7LE
Telephone:	01–374 1798
Telex:	887887
Fax:	01–374 4399

Company Details

Full-time Executives:	5
Type of Organisation:	Captive
Funds Managed:	None
Total Capital Invested:	c. £15m
Total Capital Available:	Unlimited
Specialisations:	None
Current Portfolio Size:	10
Investments as Lead Investor:	Clares Equipment Ltd; VF International Ltd.

Investment Preferences

Minimum Investment:	£500,000
Preferred Investment:	£2m
Type of Funding:	Equity/Mezzanine
Stage of Investment:	Expansion and Buy-out/Buy-in
Investment Conditions:	None
Industry Preferences:	None
Geographical Preferences:	UK/Europe

Contacts:	A.E.B. Wiegman, Managing Director (01–374 1817); R.M. Lindemann, Director (01–374 1820); N.B. Wheeler, Director (01–374 1799); C.K. Lau, Financial Controller (01–374 7585); B.H. Llovera, Executive (01–374 1894)

Company:	SECURITY PACIFIC VENTURE CAPITAL
Address:	130 Jermyn Street, London SW1Y 4UJ
Telephone:	01–925 2395
Telex:	—
Fax:	01–930 2348

Company Details

Full-time Executives:	18
Type of Organisation:	Subsidiary of Security Pacific
Funds Managed:	—
Total Capital Invested:	£150m ($250m)
Total Capital Available:	Not limited
Specialisations:	None
Current Portfolio Size:	150
Investments as Lead Investor:	Advanced Aluminium Products; HSA

Investment Preferences

Minimum Investment:	None
Preferred Investment:	£600,000 and over
Type of Funding:	Equity-driven, flexible structuring
Stage of Investment:	Start-up, Expansion, Buy-out
Investment Conditions:	None
Industry Preferences:	None
Geographical Preferences:	UK, International

Contact:	Dmitry Bosky

Company:	SEED CAPITAL LTD
Address:	Boston Road, Henley on Thames, Oxon RG9 1DY
Telephone:	(0491) 579999
Telex:	—
Fax:	(0491) 579825

Company Details

Full-time Executives:	1
Type of Organisation:	Independent
Funds Managed:	Seedcorn Capital Ltd
	Seed Investments Ltd
	Seed Investments II Ltd
Total Capital Invested:	£365,000
Total Capital Available:	£400,000
Specialisations:	Innovative engineering and electronics
Current Portfolio Size:	12
Investments as	
Lead Investor:	Bell Plastics; Select Information Systems; X-Ray Tag; PSI Atomisers; Pulse Electronics; Tribotics

Investment Preferences

Minimum Investment:	£5,000
Preferred Investment:	£25,000
Type of Funding:	Equity only
Stage of Investment:	Prototype financing, pre start-up and seed capital
Investment Conditions:	None. If the seed investments are successful, further capital may be provided by a major venture capital fund.
Industry Preferences:	Technology
Geographical Preferences:	Near Henley-on-Thames

Contact:	Lucius Cary

Company:	**SUMIT EQUITY VENTURES LIMITED** (formerly AES Equity Ventures)
Address:	Edmund House, 12 Newhall Street, Birmingham B3 3ER
Telephone:	021–200 2244
Telex:	—
Fax:	021–200 2245

Company Details

Full-time Executives:	8
Type of Organisation:	Independent
Funds Managed:	SUMIT plc
	Sharp Technology Fund PLC (STF)

Total Capital Invested:	SUMIT: £24m/STF: £7.4m
Total Capital Available:	SUMIT/STF: £35m
Specialisations:	SUMIT: General/STF: Technology related companies
Current Portfolio Size:	SUMIT: 27/STF: 16
Investments as	
Lead Investor:	Fuel Tech plc; Keep Brothers; Meatpak; Partco (co-leader); Power Centres

Investment Preferences

Minimum Investment:	SUMIT: £500,000/STF: £300,000
Preferred Investment:	SUMIT: £500,000–£1,250,000
	STF: £300,00–£600,00. Both funds will syndicate larger sums
Type of Funding:	SUMIT/STF: Equity, occasionally with supporting loans
Stage of Investment:	SUMIT: expansion, buy-out/in STF: 2nd Stage, expansion, buy-out/in
Investment Conditions:	SUMIT: Track record, strong management
	STF: Strong management
Industry Preferences:	SUMIT: No sector preference
	STF: Technology related companies
Geographical Preferences:	SUMIT/STF: UK

Contacts:	Lindsay Bury, Mike Cunnell, Jackie Horton, John Kerr, Liz Martin-Rosenfield, Nick Talbot-Rice, Nick Trigg, Caspar Weston

Company:	**SUN LIFE INVESTMENT MANAGEMENT SERVICES LTD**
Address:	107 Cheapside, London EC2V 6DU
Telephone:	01–606 7788
Telex:	268805
Fax:	01–600 3501

Company Details

Full-time Executives:	3
Type of Organisation:	Captive
Funds Managed:	Sun Life Assurance Society PLC
Total Capital Invested:	£37m
Total Capital Available:	£10m p.a.

Specialisations: None
Current Portfolio Size: 72
Investments as
  Lead Investor: —

Investment Preferences

Minimum Investment: £250,000
Preferred Investment: £1m
Type of Funding: Flexible package always including equity
Stage of Investment: Preference for Development/Expansion, MBO,
                           MBI, Acquisition and Replacement Finance
Investment Conditions: Profitable companies preferred
Industry Preferences: None
Geographical Preferences: UK

Contact: David Bays

Company: **TECHNET INVESTMENTS LIMITED**
Address: 63–67 Newington Causeway, London SE1 6BD
Telephone: 01–403 0300
Telex: —
Fax: 01–403 1742

Company Details

Full-time Executives: 8
Type of Organisation: Greater London Enterprise Group Vehicle
Funds Managed: Development Fund, Kickstart Fund
Total Capital Invested: £1.2m
Total Capital Available: £0.8m
Specialisations: Project management in all areas of technology
Current Portfolio Size: 7
Investments as
  Lead Investor: Esprit
                           Delta
                           Axiom Systems Design Ltd

Investment Preferences

Minimum Investment: £5,000 under Kickstart Fund
Preferred Investment: £10,000 Kickstart Fund
                           £100,000 Development Fund
Type of Funding: Equity, Options, Loans

Stage of Investment:	Most stages
Investment Conditions:	No specific conditions but minimum rate of return necessary
Industry Preferences:	All areas of Technology
Geographical Preferences:	Greater London Area

Contacts:	Clive Bridges (Technology Director); Denis Clench (Technology Manager); Bianca Hallion, Alan Doggett (Technology Executives)

Company:	**THE ST JAMES'S VENTURE CAPITAL FUND LIMITED**
Address:	15 St. James's Place, London SW1A 1NW
Telephone:	01–431 4381
Telex:	883625
Fax:	01–431 2531

Company Details

Full-time Executives:	4
Type of Organisation:	Venture Capital subsidiary of RIT Capital Partners plc
Funds Managed:	The St James's Venture Capital Fund Ltd
Total Capital Invested:	£8.5m
Total Capital Available:	Unspecified
Specialisations:	Technology, industrial automation, optoelectronics, microelectronics, health care and biotechnology
Current Portfolio Size:	15
Investments as Lead Investor:	Insignia Solutions Limited

Investment Preferences

Minimum Investment:	£250,000
Preferred Investment:	£750,000
Type of Funding:	Equity with or without loan
Stage of Investment:	All stages
Investment Conditions:	One year sales history
Industry Preferences:	Technology
Geographical Preferences:	UK, Europe, USA

Contact:	Dr S. Hochhauser

Company:	THOMPSON CLIVE & PARTNERS LIMITED
Address:	24 Old Bond Street, London W1X 3DA
Telephone:	01–491 4809
Telex:	8953833
Fax:	01–493 9172

Company Details

Full-time Executives:	8
Type of Organisation:	Independent
Funds Managed:	Thompson Clive Investments plc
	Thompson Clive Growth Companies Fund
	Thompson Clive Ventures
Total Capital Invested:	£58m
Total Capital Available:	£20m
Specialisations:	Systems, Electronics, Health Care, Biotechnology, Service Businesses
Current Portfolio Size:	44
Investments as	
Lead Investor:	International Colour Management plc; Isotron plc; Universal Health Care plc; Drew Scientific Ltd; Sifam Ltd

Investment Preferences

Minimum Investment:	None
Preferred Investment:	£500,000–£2m
Type of Funding:	Equity
Stage of Investment:	All stages
Investment Conditions:	None
Industry Preferences:	Systems, Electronics, Health Care, Biotechnology, Services Businesses, Professional and Industrial Markets
Geographical Preferences:	UK, USA, France

Contacts:	Stephen Black, Nat Hone
	Alternatively: David Bailey, Colin Clive, Charles Fitzherbert, Robin Meyer, Richard Thompson

Company:	TRANSATLANTIC CAPITAL LTD
Address:	65 Holborn Viaduct, London EC1A 2EU
Telephone:	01–489 0021

Telex:	886653 PROCUR G
Fax:	01–248 1103

Company Details

Full-time Executives:	3
Type of Organisation:	Independent
Funds Managed:	Transatlantic Capital Bio-Sciences Fund
	Partnership A
	Partnership B
Total Capital Invested:	£2.5m
Total Capital Available:	£5m
Specialisations:	Bio-sciences including medical, healthcare, bio-technology and related industries
Current Portfolio Size:	10
Investments as	
Lead Investor:	Alliance Imaging PLC; Ethical Pharmaceuticals Ltd; Automated Microbiology Systems Ltd

Investment Preferences

Minimum Investment:	£50,000
Preferred Investment:	£250,000
Type of Funding:	Equity with loan
Stage of Investment:	Seed Capital, Start-up, Expansion, Development and Buy-out
Investment Conditions:	Proprietary technology or unique market opportunity
Industry Preferences:	Bio-sciences
Geographical Preferences:	UK, Europe, USA

Contacts:	Gordon Dean, Paul Frampton, Fred Offer

Company:	**ULSTER DEVELOPMENT CAPITAL LIMITED**
Address:	1 Arthur Street, Belfast BT1 4GA
Telephone:	Belfast (0232) 246765
Telex:	—
Fax:	(0232) 232982

Company Details

Full-time Executives:	3
Type of Organisation:	Independent

Funds Managed:	N/A
Total Capital Invested:	£1.1m
Total Capital Available:	£0.8m
Specialisations:	General
Current Portfolio Size:	8
Investments as	
Lead Investor:	Meltan Packaging (NI) Limited; Nectar Cosmetics Limited

Investment Preferences

Minimum Investment:	£50,000
Preferred Investment:	£50,000–£300,000
Type of Funding:	Equity only
Stage of Investment:	Expansion and Buy-out
Investment Conditions:	Minimum potential profit of £100,000 in short term
Industry Preferences:	None
Geographical Preferences:	Northern Ireland

Contacts:	Edmund W. Johnston, Rodney C. Johnston, Daniel R. McIlwrath

Company:	**VENTURE FOUNDERS LIMITED**
Address:	West Court, Salamander Quay, Harefield, Uxbridge, Middlesex UB9 6NZ
Telephone:	(0895) 824015
Telex:	—
Fax:	(0895) 823099

Company Details

Full-time Executives:	4
Type of Organisation:	Independent
Funds Managed:	The Venture Founders Fund
	Venture Founders Capital Limited Fund
Total Capital Invested:	£12m
Total Capital Available:	£6m
Specialisations:	Information technologies, transportation, computer peripherals, software and medical
Current Portfolio Size:	32

Investments as
   Lead Investor: Softbridge Microsystems (UK) Ltd; Xenova Ltd; Technology Services International Ltd; International Communications Group Ltd

Investment Preferences

Minimum Investment:	£100,000
Preferred Investment:	£250,000–£600,000
Type of Funding:	Equity
Stage of Investment:	Start-up and Expansion
Investment Conditions:	Developed product or service
Industry Preferences:	All industrial, technological and service sectors
Geographical Preferences:	UK, Europe, U.S.A.

Contacts: J.M. Frye, A.T. Brocklebank, A.F. Ryden

Company:	**VENTURE LINK INVESTORS LTD**
Address:	Tectonic Place, Holyport Road, Maidenhead, Berkshire SL6 2YG
Telephone:	0628 771050
Telex:	—
Fax:	0628 770392

Company Details

Full-time Executives:	5
Type of Organisation:	Independent
Funds Managed:	Venture Link M4 Syndicate
	Venture Link Software Syndicate
Total Capital Invested:	£9m
Total Capital Available:	£21m
Specialisations:	Electronics (especially software), biotechnology and health-care
Current Portfolio Size:	15

Investments as
   Lead Investor: Century Hutchinson Ltd; C.L.E.A.R. (Holdings) Ltd; Manufacturing Management Ltd; Systematica Ltd; Unisoft Group Ltd

Investment Preferences

Minimum Investment:	£200,000
Preferred Investment:	£200,000–£400,000 (initially)

Type of Funding:	Equity related
Stage of Investment:	Start-up and follow-on
Investment Conditions:	Excellent management team
Industry Preferences:	Most considered
Geographical Preferences:	UK (especially M4 corridor)

Contacts:	John V. Hatch (Managing Director); Hilary J. Marsh (Director); Anthony G. Parkes (Director)

Company:	**WELSH DEVELOPMENT AGENCY**
Address:	Pearl House, Greyfriars Road, Cardiff CF1 3XX
Telephone:	(0222) 222666
Telex:	497513
Fax:	(0222) 223243

Company Details

Full-time Executives:	35
Type of Organisation:	Statutory Government Body
Funds Managed:	Welsh Development Agency Investment Funds
Total Capital Invested:	£35m
Total Capital Available:	Open
Specialisations:	None
Current Portfolio Size:	500
Investments as	
Lead Investor:	—

Investment Preferences

Minimum Investment:	None
Preferred Investment:	Under £500,000 for first round finance
Type of Funding:	Equity only or Equity with loan
Stage of Investment:	All stages considered
Investment Conditions:	All potentially viable propositions considered
Industry Preferences:	All sectors except media, local retail and agriculture
Geographical Preferences:	Wales only

Contact:	Keith Williams, Investment Director

Company:	**WELSH DEVELOPMENT CAPITAL (MANAGEMENT) LIMITED**
Address:	Pearl House, Greyfriars Road, Cardiff CF1 3XX
Telephone:	(0222) 378531

Telex:	497513
Fax:	(0222) 223243

Company Details

Full-time Executives:	3
Type of Organisation:	Independent
Funds Managed:	Welsh Venture Capital Fund
Total Capital Invested:	£4m
Total Capital Available:	£1.5m
Specialisations:	None
Current Portfolio Size:	14
Investments as	
Lead Investor:	—

Investment Preferences

Minimum Investment:	£100,000
Preferred Investment:	£100,000–£300,000
Type of Funding:	Equity only and Equity with loan
Stage of Investment:	All stages except seed capital
Investment Conditions:	Strong growth potential
Industry Preferences:	None
Geographical Preferences:	Wales

Contacts:	Alan Jones, Colin Morris

Company:	**WEST MIDLANDS ENTERPRISE BOARD LIMITED**
Address:	31–34 Waterloo Street, Birmingham B2 5TJ
Telephone:	021–236 8855
Telex:	—
Fax:	021–233 3942

Company Details

Full-time Executives:	8
Type of Organisation:	Independent venture capital company responsible to West Midlands District Councils
Funds Managed:	The West Midlands Regional Unit Trust West Midlands Enterprise Board
Total Capital Invested:	£12m
Total Capital Available:	£8m
Specialisations:	General

Current Portfolio Size:	34
Investments as	
Lead Investor:	Docker Foods Ltd

Investment Preferences

Minimum Investment:	£100,000. Also manages local Venture Capital Funds investing £25/50,000 in smaller companies
Preferred Investment:	£200,000–£700,000
Type of Funding:	Equity/Loan
Stage of Investment:	Larger start-ups/expansion/MBO/MBI
Investment Conditions:	Minimum potential internal rate of return of 25%
Industry Preferences:	Most manufacturing and productive service industries
Geographical Preferences:	Hereford & Worcester, Oxfordshire, Shropshire, Staffordshire, Warwickshire, West Midlands County

Contacts:	Peter Collings, Keith Wilkinson

Company:	**YORKSHIRE ENTERPRISE LIMITED**
Address:	Elizabeth House, Queen Street, Leeds LS1 2TW
Telephone:	0532 420505
Telex:	556131
Fax:	0532 420266

Company Details

Full-time Executives:	9
Type of Organisation:	Independent
Funds Managed:	Barnsley Investments Limited, Bradford, Metropolitan Enterprises Limited, Calderdale Metropolitan Investments Limited, Humberside County Enterprises Limited, North Yorkshire Investment Company Limited, Sheffield City Investments Limited
Total Capital Invested:	£13m
Total Capital Available:	£15m
Specialisations:	General
Current Portfolio Size:	71
Investments as	
Lead Investor:	Hotwork International; Optare; Willoughby Layne Group; Crystal Drinks; South Riding Video and TV Productions

Investment Preferences

Minimum Investment:	£25,000
Preferred Investment:	Full range to £2m +
Type of Funding:	Equity and Loan
Stage of Investment:	Start-ups, expansions, MBO's, MBI's, reconstructions
Investment Conditions:	None
Industry Preferences:	None
Geographical Preferences:	Yorkshire & Humberside
Contact:	Donald Law, Director of Investment

This Appendix is reproduced with kind permission of the BVCA from the 1990 Directory of Members. The *BVCA Directory of Full and Associate Members* (which is published annually) is available free of charge from the BVCA Secretariat, 1 Surrey Street, London WC2R 2PS. Telephone: 01-836 5702

Index